BASKETBALL BIOGRAPHIES FOR KIDS

BASKETBALL BIOGRAPHIES

FOR KIDS

STORIES OF BASKETBALL'S MOST INSPIRING PLAYERS

MATT CHANDLER

Illustrations by
BRENNA DAUGHERTY

callisto
publishing
an imprint of Sourcebooks

Published by Callisto Publishing LLC C/O Sourcebooks LLC
P.O. Box 4410, Naperville, Illinois 60567-4410
(630) 961-3900
callistopublishing.com

Originally published as *Basketball Biographies for Kids* in 2022 in the United States of
America by Callisto Kids, an imprint of Sourcebooks. This edition issued based on the
paperback edition published in 2022 in the United States of America by Callisto Kids,
an imprint of Sourcebooks.

This product conforms to all applicable CPSC and CPSIA standards.

Source of Production: Versa Press
Date of Production: January 2024
Run Number: 5037428

Printed and bound in the United States of America.
VP 10 9 8 7 6 5 4 3 2 1

To Amber, Zoey, and Oliver:
My best friend, my Zee Duck, and my
favorite basketball player.

I couldn't do any of this
without Team Chandler.

☆ ☆ ☆

CONTENTS

INTRODUCTION

At five feet, seven inches tall, I wasn't destined to have a career in basketball—at least not in the traditional sense. Growing up, I could hold my own in a game of HORSE or Around the World, but I had no dreams of one day playing point guard for my hometown team, the Boston Celtics. Still, in a different sense I did develop a basketball career, as a writer.

I began my career covering high school sports as a freelance journalist. It was there that I got my first serious up close and personal view of the game of basketball. Sitting in a high school gym on a Friday night watching two teams battle it out is a great way to learn the game. Years later, when I became a children's book author, I put what I learned in those early years to good use.

This is my seventh basketball book. In writing each one, I have developed a deeper appreciation for the game of basketball and the men and women who play it at the highest level. It is this appreciation, and passion, for the game that I hope comes through these pages and gets you excited.

Have you ever debated with your friends or family who the best players in the game are? Have you imagined that you are a general manager, and you get to assemble a dream team of the best players in the National Basketball Association (NBA) or Women's National Basketball Association (WNBA)? That is exactly what this book is.

I have put together my dream team of the best player from each position in the NBA and in the WNBA. Ten chapters, ten players. The best center, point guard, shooting guard, power forward, and small forward from each league, together on one team. And, because choosing the best is open to debate, I have included three honorable mentions for each position as well. Finally, no basketball book would be complete without revisiting some of the players that built the game. The game has evolved so much over the years. The players are bigger, faster, and stronger. The rules and strategies have evolved. Basketball players of today could not truly compare to the superstars of a generation or more ago. That's why you'll find a "legend" for each position included as well.

After you read this book, I hope you come away feeling a spark of excitement for the game. I hope you come to appreciate the contributions these players have made both on and off the court and I hope you learn a thing or two (or ten) along the way!

I also hope you use this book to start conversations with your friends and family. Nothing livens up the dinner conversation more than arguing who the best players in the league are. Debate who on my list is over-rated, argue who I missed, and discuss what you think would happen if some of the legends in the book squared off against today's superstars. Could Michael Jordan outshine Steph Curry? Would Larry Bird get the better of LeBron James? Make your own lists, argue in support of your own players, and develop your own dream teams.

Most of all, I hope you have fun reading this book. Whether it is the electricity of sitting courtside for Game 7 of the NBA Finals or the excitement as Diana Taurasi becomes the all-time leading scorer in WNBA history, I hope you feel the magic reading this book that I felt writing it.

WHY THEY WERE PICKED

First, let's begin with acknowledging that picking the best person in any group is nothing more than an opinion. How is *greatness* defined? Most of you have never heard of Dickey Simpkins, for example, even though he won three NBA titles. Does that mean he is great? Not necessarily. It means he was a reserve—meaning he was a substitute player who often didn't play at all—on the Chicago Bulls dynasty of the 1990s. So, he was a player in the right place at the right time. Charles Barkley didn't win a single NBA Championship title in his 17-year career. Does that mean he wasn't a good player? Of course not. "Sir Charles," as he was nicknamed, was an 11-time All-Star, a league Most Valuable Player (MVP), an Olympic gold medalist, and is enshrined in the Basketball Hall of Fame.

In the following chapters you'll read about players who may not always be the statistically best at their positions. They may not have a championship ring for every finger, but they may have the "it" factor of greatness.

The NBA has been overflowing with incredible talent for decades. Today, the NBA and WNBA rosters include over 500 active players combined. Narrowing those numbers down to 10 total players was a daunting task. To do so, I looked at a combination of factors, including length of career, number of playoff appearances, championships won, individual accolades (All-Star Team selections, scoring titles, etc.), and the impact the player has had not only on his or her team, but also on the league and on the community outside of basketball.

Players who didn't quite make the cut were given consideration as honorable mentions. The legendary greats were measured using similar criteria as the current players. In the end, I measured the final selections based on one simple idea: If I were a general manager and had to win a single game, and I could assemble the best players to field a single team, who would I choose? These are my dream teams, and I feel pretty good saying they would be unbeatable in a single game.

TERMS, PHRASES, AND ACRONYMS

Around the World: A game where players have to shoot (and make) baskets from set points around the key on the basketball court

alley-oop pass: When a player tosses the ball to another player who is in the air and then scores with it

assists: A statistic that is counted when a player passes the ball to another player who then scores

blocks: A statistic that is counted when a player legally blocks an offensive member of the opposite team from scoring

bucket: A slang term for making a basket that scores two or three points

center: The position for the tallest person on the team. They play near the basket and focus on rebounds and close shots.

deflect: When a player hits part of the ball, does not get possession, but gets it away from the opponent. This is not a traditionally counted stat.

dribble: The act of bouncing the ball off the floor to move around the basketball court. It is a violation of the rules for a player to move the ball without dribbling or passing.

drive the lane: To dribble while charging toward the hoop to take a layup

dunk (or slam dunk): A shot where the player jumps in the air and uses their hands to push the ball into the basket over the basket's rim

fadeaway jump shot: A jump shot taken by the player while jumping backwards

free throw: An unopposed shot from the free-throw line, usually given after the opposite team makes a foul

hook shot: A shot where a player, usually turned sideways to the basket, uses their arm furthest from the basket to throw over their head

HORSE: A game of five shots each where a player must repeat the shot style of the first player

inbounds pass: Passing the ball from out-of-bounds to a player who is inbounds

layup: A shot that is made near the basket. It usually bounces off the backboard of the hoop to get into the basket.

opening tip-off: When the referee throws up the ball between two players to start a basketball game

point guard: The position on the team for the person who is typically the best dribbler and passer. This player runs the offense and defends against the opposite team's point guard.

power forward: The position on the team that is similar to the center. This player also plays near the basket, but generally they take longer shots than the center.

PPG (Points Per Game): A stat that shows the average points per game a player scores

rebound: Gaining possession of a ball after a missed shot, also known as *boards*. A *defensive rebound* is a ball taken when the other team misses a shot. An *offensive rebound* is a ball taken when the player's own team misses a shot.

regulation: The set time of a basketball game without going into overtime. NBA games are set at 48 minutes. WNBA games are 40 minutes. Neither of these times include when the clock is stopped for fouls, halftime, or time-outs.

reserve: A substitute player who doesn't play often, if at all, in a game

RPG (Rebounds Per Game): A stat that shows the average rebounds per game a player has taken

set a screen: When an offensive player attempts to block a player on the opposite team who is guarding the offensive player's teammate

shooting guard: This is the position for the team's best shooter. Their main goal is to score points and steal the ball from the opposite team.

shot clock: The clock that counts down how long a player has to shoot the ball. In both the WNBA and the NBA, a player has 24 seconds.

sky hook: A hook shot, considered perfected by Kareem Abdul-Jabar, where the player jumps before throwing

small forward: The position on the team that's in the middle height-wise between the center and guards; they are responsible for scoring and defending but also grabbing rebounds and handling the ball.

steals: A statistic that is counted when a player takes possession of the ball from an offensive player, usually while dribbling or during a pass

three-pointer: A shot taken from behind the three-point line, about 22 feet from the basket for the NBA and 20 feet for the WNBA and international play

top of the key: The space in between the three-point line and the free-throw line

triple-double: A score of at least 10 in three of the main stat categories, such as points, rebounds, assists, or blocks

JOEL EMBIID

NBA CENTER

BIRTH YEAR	1994
BIRTHPLACE	YAOUNDÉ, CAMEROON
HEIGHT | WEIGHT	7'0" | 280 LBS
YEARS ACTIVE	2014–PRESENT
TEAMS	PHILADELPHIA 76ERS

CAREER STATISTICS

(THROUGH THE 2022-23 SEASON)

394
GAMES PLAYED

10,718
POINTS

4,402
REBOUNDS

1,354
ASSISTS

654
BLOCKS

AWARDS

BIG 12 DEFENSIVE PLAYER OF THE YEAR, 2014;
NBA ALL-STAR, 2018, 2019, 2020, 2021, 2022, 2023

A FIRST CHOICE PLAYER

Every basketball game begins with the center. From winning the opening tip-off—the jump ball that begins the game—and setting some early energy, to controlling the boards and wearing out the opposing players, the center is the heart of any successful team.

If the NBA were to add a new team today, a team that was able to select any players it wanted, Joel Embiid would likely be the center of choice. Embiid, the carefree spirit of the Philadelphia 76ers, may not have the eye-popping stats of some of the other centers in the NBA, and he is still waiting on his first championship ring, but he offers a mix of qualities that make him the best pure center in the NBA today.

A DOMINATING FIRST PLAYOFF

Four years after he played his last college game as a Kansas Jayhawk, Embiid took to the court for an NBA Playoff game. However, like much of his NBA career, his playoff experience was delayed by injury. Just a couple weeks before the start of the postseason, Embiid collided with one of his own teammates and he suffered a broken bone near his left eye. When the playoffs began with the 76ers facing the Miami Heat, Embiid had to sit out the first two games, setting up a dramatic playoff debut for him in Game 3.

Like all the greats, he was at his best under pressure, with the game on the line. In the fourth quarter, with just under five and a half minutes left to play, Philadelphia was clinging to a seven-point lead. Then Embiid took over. Catching a quick pass, he dribbled through the other players, completed a nifty spin move, and tossed up the ball, banging it off the glass and into the basket. For a point guard it would have been an impressive shot. For a seven-foot center, it was stunning.

But Embiid wasn't done yet. On the next possession, teammate Dario Šarić sent Embiid a pass to the far side of the court. Embiid went up and over six-foot-eight Heat forward James Johnson like he wasn't even there, making a three-point shot and extending the lead to 12 points. He added seven rebounds and the Sixers won. At the end of the game, Embiid led all scoring with 23 points. Still, Embiid remained focused on the big picture.

FAST FACTS

- Started playing organized basketball at the age of 16

- Drafted No. 3 overall in 2014

- In the 2018-2019 season, became the third player to average at least 27 PPG and 13 RPG

"I was sad I couldn't play in the first game. We went through a lot, and to be able to be in this position, I'm really happy," he said in his postgame press conference. "But we can't be satisfied, we've got a big one [Game 4] on Saturday."

That focus was critical. Embiid, who averaged more than 20 points in each game, led the 76ers to win the series, 4–1.

FROM CAMEROON TO FLORIDA

Joel Embiid was born in Cameroon, Africa, a country of 25 million people on the Gulf of Guinea. He is the oldest of three children, and grew up watching over his younger siblings.

As a young boy, Embiid had no plans to play basketball. The sport was so rare in his native country that there were only two public courts. Instead, his father pushed him to pursue a career in volleyball. By the time he was 15, Embiid was nearly seven feet tall, so becoming a forceful hitter in volleyball made perfect sense. Luckily, for basketball fans around the world, that never happened. Embiid soon followed another path, one that would lead him to the NBA.

Most NBA greats have played basketball their entire lives. LeBron James, for example, was just nine years old when he suited up for his first team. Klay Thompson, of the Golden State Warriors, learned the game from his father's teammates on the Los Angeles Lakers when he was barely able to walk. For Embiid, it was different. It wasn't until he was 15 years old that he began to play the game that has now brought him so much fame and success.

During a youth basketball camp, Embiid met Luc Richard Mbah a Moute, a native of Cameroon. Mbah a Moute was drafted by the Milwaukee Bucks in 2008. During the off-season, Mbah a Moute returned to Cameroon to host basketball clinics. It was at one of those clinics that he discovered Joel Embiid.

Embiid's size and strength, especially for someone so young, stood out to Mbah a Moute right away. He convinced Embiid's parents that their son had a future in basketball. With Mbah a Moute as his mentor, Embiid moved to the United States and enrolled in the same Florida high school that the Bucks power forward had. He was firmly under the wing of Mbah a Moute and on the radar of professional scouts. He didn't know it at the time, but Embiid was less than three years away from signing his first professional basketball contract!

It's important to note that the odds of making it to the NBA are astronomical. And that's if you live and play in the United States, where the game is so popular. For a young player who barely spoke English, living in a country nearly 7,000 miles away and picking up a basketball for the first time as a teenager, the odds would appear impossible. That didn't stop Embiid.

COMPETING IN THE PROS

After high school, Embiid attended the University of Kansas, where he joined the Jayhawks basketball team. He immediately became an impact player in the 2013–14 season, averaging 11 points and more than 2.5 blocks per game his freshman year. The Jayhawks made it into the National Collegiate Athletic Association (NCAA) tournament, but an injury kept Embiid on the bench. At the end of the season, he faced a tough decision: Should he return to Kansas and improve his prospects for joining the NBA after he graduated? Or should he join the growing number of players who left college teams to join the pros as soon as possible? In April 2014, Embiid answered that question, announcing he was leaving Kansas and declaring himself eligible for the NBA draft.

Though he suffered a pre-draft injury to his foot, Embiid was still selected third overall by the Philadelphia 76ers. It took Embiid two years to finally get fully healthy and ready to play for the team.

Embiid used his time on the injured list to study the game. At 20 years old, he had only been playing basketball for five years and had just a single year of Division I college experience. Embiid's time on the injured reserve list gave him an opportunity to watch game film, study opponents, attend team meetings, and involve himself in the game in a way that wouldn't have been possible if he were grinding out an 82-game season.

In the 2016–17 season, when he was finally able to participate, he was only put on the court for 31 games. Even in that limited role, he averaged 20 points per game and showed flashes of the brilliance that led the 76ers to draft him in the first round.

His biggest night as a pro came on December 18, 2016, when the Sixers hosted the Brooklyn Nets. Embiid managed to score a career high of 33 points in the game, including a pair of free throws with 12 seconds left in the fourth quarter that helped seal a 108–107 win for the hometown team.

Though his high scoring and rebounding were crucial to the win, it was a play that didn't show up on the stat sheets that energized his team and the fans. Early in the fourth quarter, with the Sixers trailing by one point, Embiid deflected a pass and the ball headed out of bounds. Embiid launched his seven-foot frame into the air, vaulting over the first row of fans and swatting the ball back to the court. As he landed in the second row, the fans held their collective breath. When their star rose from the seats and climbed back onto the court, the crowd erupted into cheers. The fans in the stands recognized he was more than just a shooter or a rebounder: He was a competitor willing to do whatever it took to win the game.

DRIVEN TO SUCCEED

As a first-round draft pick, Embiid was expected to begin a career as a consistent All-Star. But before his first season even started, Embiid found out he had a bone fracture in his right foot that would require surgery. The good news was that the 76ers still chose to draft and sign him despite the injury. The bad news was that he would miss his entire rookie season. His dream would have to wait while he healed.

For a young player just two years out of high school, the situation was especially challenging. Embiid was being paid more than $4 million by the Sixers, but he couldn't even play! Any other player might have been tempted to slack off, to get caught up in his newfound riches and let his game get worse. Instead, Embiid focused on healing his body and getting stronger. He was determined to come back better than ever for the 2015–16 season.

Then, disaster struck again. Embiid broke the same bone in his right foot and the team had to announce that he would miss his second consecutive season. The 76ers believed it was potentially a career-ending injury. With more than $8 million in guaranteed salary and another year of painful rehab facing him, Embiid could have let his dream slip away.

Instead, he fought. He persevered. He worked out, stayed in basketball shape, and allowed his foot to heal. It took him nearly three years from his last game at Kansas to play in his first game in the NBA. But Joel Embiid never quit. He never let his bad fortune define him or defeat him, and in 2023, he won the league MVP trophy. He proved he was a warrior, and in doing so, he offered a valuable lesson to every young fan watching the NBA: Follow your dreams, and never, ever give up.

BRITTNEY GRINER

WNBA CENTER

BIRTH YEAR	1990
BIRTHPLACE	HOUSTON, TEXAS
HEIGHT | WEIGHT	6'9" | 205 LBS
YEARS ACTIVE	2013–PRESENT
TEAMS	PHOENIX MERCURY, ZHEJIANG GOLDEN BULLS, UMMC EKATERINBURG

CAREER STATISTICS
(THROUGH THE 2023 SEASON)

285
GAMES PLAYED

5,038
POINTS

2,125
REBOUNDS

531
ASSISTS

766
BLOCKS

AWARDS

WNBA CHAMPION, 2014; WNBA ALL-STAR, 2013–2015, 2017–2023; NCAA FINAL FOUR MOST OUTSTANDING PLAYER; ASSOCIATED PRESS PLAYER OF THE YEAR, 2012; DEFENSIVE PLAYER OF THE YEAR, 2014, 2015

THE DEFINITION OF SUPERSTAR

In all of professional basketball history, no center other than Brittney Griner has been a leading scorer for more than two decades. The Phoenix Mercury center has won the WNBA scoring title twice—in 2017 and 2019—and she added two Defensive Player of the Year awards along the way.

Her dominance as a scorer, as a physical presence on the court, and as a strong defender dates back to her college years at Baylor University, where Griner became the first player in NCAA women's basketball history to score 2,000 points and record 500 blocks. Griner was a four-year superstar at Baylor on both sides of the ball, meaning she played both offense and defense. She won countless national awards and lead Baylor to the National Championship as a junior in 2012. In the history of NCAA basketball, for both men and women, no one has more career blocks than the 736 on Griner's resume.

In the seven years since the Phoenix Mercury selected her first in the WNBA Draft, Griner has proven herself to be not only the most successful center in the league but also, arguably, in the history of the WNBA.

THE OLYMPICS AT LAST

On August 20, 2016, Brittney Griner proudly stood on the top tier of an awards podium 5,000 miles from home,

FAST FACTS

- No. 1 pick in the 2013 WNBA Draft

- Seven-time All Star

- First WNBA player to dunk twice in one game

- One of only 11 players in the world who have earned an Olympic gold medal, International Basketball Federation (FIBA) World Cup gold medal, WNBA title, and NCAA title

where she and Team USA had just won the gold medal for basketball at the Olympics. She beamed as she held the medallion tight, a symbol of all she had overcome in her career and in her life.

Griner is one of the most decorated college basketball players in history and has earned plenty of trophies and awards in her WNBA career. But most athletes will tell you that there is something special, something almost magical, about representing your country in the Olympic Games. And for Griner, it was an opportunity she had passed up once before, making this experience all the sweeter.

In 2012, Griner was slated to be chosen as the lone college player to join the US women's basketball team in the London Olympics. But she withdrew her name just before the team was announced, saying her mother's illness and schoolwork were the reasons she couldn't join the team. It was a huge decision for a college student to make: Walking away from the chance to represent her country as part of a team that was heavily favored to win the gold medal.

"I am disappointed that I will be unable to participate," Griner said at the time of the announcement. "I want to stay involved in USA Basketball and hope to have the opportunity to represent my country in future international competition."

By the time the 2016 Rio Games rolled around, Griner had established herself as one of the most dominant centers in the WNBA and was a shoo-in to become a member of Team USA. She was of course selected, and, as they did in 2012, the US women's team rolled through the Olympics with relative ease, winning the gold medal. Griner had posted 78 points and 47 rebounds in eight games. In an interview from Rio, Griner talked about what it was like for her to finally be an Olympian.

"I love it. It's just different than playing in the WNBA. We're playing on the biggest stage possible. You're playing for your country," she said at the time. "Being around all these great players, it brings out the best in you."

IT STARTED IN HIGH SCHOOL

Brittney Griner was born and raised in Houston, Texas, one of four children. As a child, Griner had no interest in basketball or sports in general. Instead, she describes herself as a "daddy's girl" who preferred to help her dad work on the family car, a fascination she still has today.

"[I] loved being out there changing oil and tires with him," Griner wrote in a *Sports Illustrated Kids* essay. "My dad wanted to teach me those things, so I wouldn't always have to depend on others. Even now, I'll help a friend out if they have car trouble."

When Griner showed an interest in sports as a seventh grader, she gravitated toward volleyball and soccer. Her height and long arms made her a natural on the volleyball court.

After her freshman year, coaches convinced Griner that she had the talent to play basketball. She quit volleyball and focused her efforts on what was for her a completely foreign game. Unlike many players for whom basketball comes naturally, Griner described her early experience learning the game as incredibly challenging.

"I was so lost," Griner once wrote of her first year playing basketball. "Coach would say, 'Set a screen,' but I didn't know what a screen was!"

Her former high school coach, Debbie Jackson, told *USA Today* that once Griner dunked the ball in a regular season game, everything changed. "After word got out that she was dunking the ball, we had 15 college coaches in the gym watching practice the next day," Jackson said. After two years playing high school basketball, Griner began considering a future in the sport. She had grown to over six feet tall and would later graduate high school at six feet, two inches.

Griner began her senior year by blocking 25 shots in the season's opening game. Her relentless hard work, focus, and determination eventually earned her a scholarship to take her talents 200 miles north to Baylor University in Waco, Texas.

SMOOTH MOVE TO THE PROS

In 2013, Griner was widely considered the greatest NCAA women's basketball player in the country. With that kind of attention comes pressure that often hurts a player, especially as she moves from college to professional ball. For Griner, however, the transition from the Baylor Lady Bears to the WNBA's Phoenix Mercury was fairly smooth.

She launched her WNBA career at home against the Chicago Sky. Veteran Diana Taurasi opened the game with a long three-point attempt. The shot ended with the ball rattling off the rim. Griner glided through to rebound, using one hand to push the ball back into the basket for the first points of the game and of her professional career. She followed that by immediately recording her first professional block on the other end of the court. The rookie finished her debut game with 17 points, eight rebounds, and a pair of monster dunks, much to the delight of the home crowd. Griner finished the season averaging 12 points and three blocks a game, sending the Mercury on a return trip to the playoffs.

In the 2014–15 season, Griner built on her rookie success, starting all 34 games for the Mercury. She raised her scoring average to 15.6 points per game (PPG) and totaled nearly four blocks per game as the Mercury finished with a 29–5 regular season record, eventually sweeping the Chicago Sky to capture the WNBA Championship. Following the game, Griner held the trophy courtside and talked about the experience of winning her first professional championship.

"The fight, and everything we had to do to get this win, it was all worth it to hold this trophy!"

A GLOBAL ADVOCATE

Griner has talked frequently about being bullied as a child. She grew up being taller than most of the boys in school. She was a tomboy—she preferred playing with G. I. Joe over Barbie. As a result, Griner's classmates regularly made fun of her.

"When I was younger, it really bothered me," Griner told the *L.A. Times*. "But as I got older, I started caring less . . . I've learned to love myself."

Griner said much of the bullying centered around people mocking her about being a girl, claiming only a man could dunk a basketball. She also faced racial taunts during games and on social media. Even though she was frequently bullied during her life, just before the WNBA draft, Griner made a bold decision: She announced that she was gay. The announcement led to a whole new level of harassment. Still, she has no regrets about her decision to open up about her personal life. With it, she says, came a chance to advocate for young people who are struggling with their own challenges.

"Don't worry about what other people are going to say, because they're always going to say something," she said in an interview with ESPN. "If you're just true to yourself, let that shine through. Don't hide who you really are."

That attitude has made Griner a role model for young people. It has cemented her legacy as an anti-bullying advocate and supporter of the Lesbian, Gay, Bisexual, Trans, Queer, Intersex, and Asexual (LGBTQIA+) community, extending her reach from the basketball court to a worldwide audience.

In February of 2022, Griner went through an extremely challenging ordeal when she was arrested and wrongfully detained in Russia for ten months. This was grueling for Griner both physically and mentally, but she persevered and was released in December of 2022. Not one to give up, Griner regained her strength and returned to the WNBA in May of 2023. She received a standing ovation at her first game.

Honorable Mentions CENTER

ANTHONY DAVIS

When the New Orleans Hornets made him the first overall selection in the 2012 NBA Draft, they knew that Anthony Davis would be a force to be reckoned with. In his career, the big man has earned eight All-Star appearances, collecting the All-Star Game Most Valuable Player Award in 2017. He has averaged more than 24 points per game each season and saved his best basketball for the postseason, where he has poured in more than 25 points a game. Still, for all his success in New Orleans, which included signing a five-year, $145-million contract in 2015, he knew he could achieve more.

In the spring of 2019, the sports world was buzzing with speculation about where Davis would be traded. One thing was clear: He wanted to take his considerable talents to a bigger market. The Los Angeles Lakers came calling. To make room, the Lakers traded away their headlining first-round pick, Lonzo Ball, seasoned players Brandon Ingram and Josh Hart, and three future first-round draft picks. Paired with LeBron James, Los Angeles clearly had its sights on bringing the NBA Championship back to Southern California. In 2020, they succeeded, and Davis won his first NBA Championship.

NIKOLA JOKIĆ

The man they call "Joker" has carved out a spot among the best centers in the NBA during his eight-year career with the Denver Nuggets. Drafted in the second round of the 2014 NBA Draft (39 spots after Joel Embiid), Jokić has steadily improved each season, posting career numbers in the 2018–19 season, including 20.1 points and nearly 11 rebounds per game. Those numbers were good enough to earn Jokić his first trip to the 2019 All-Star Game and justified the $148-million contract the Nuggets gave him before the season started. Since 2021, Jokić has won two league MVP trophies, an NBA Championship, and an NBA Finals MVP trophy.

Outside of his NBA career, Jokić represented his native Serbia in the 2016 Summer Olympics in Rio. He led the squad in rebounds, steals, and blocks per game. The Serbs advanced to the gold-medal game, where they lost to the United States, earning Jokić and his teammates a silver medal.

SYLVIA FOWLES

Greatness can be measured in many different ways. For Sylvia Fowles, greatness is measured in her performances on the biggest stage, when the spotlight is shining the brightest. In college, Fowles led the LSU Lady Tigers to the Final Four in each of her four seasons. She has also anchored four gold-medal teams at the Olympics and appeared in the WNBA Playoffs in nine consecutive years, averaging 15 points per game and 9.8 rebounds. The ability to perform her best in the biggest moments has earned Fowles two WNBA Finals MVP awards and one league MVP trophy. She retired in 2022.

Legendary Great **CENTER**

KAREEM ABDUL-JABBAR

The most exciting moment of the 1989 NBA Finals was when a player shot the ball, bouncing off the glass, and scored late in the fourth quarter. That player was Los Angeles Lakers center Kareem Abdul-Jabbar. His team was close to being beaten by the Detroit Pistons, but the bucket shot by Abdul-Jabbar was way bigger than the game. It wasn't just about the final score—it signaled the end of an era. After 20 seasons in the NBA, Abdul-Jabbar retired as the all-time leading regular season scorer in the history of the game, with 38,387 points. His record stood for 38 years.

As he completed his final NBA game, the crowd rose to its feet and cheered loudly. Abdul-Jabbar's greatness was such that every member of the Detroit Pistons stood and applauded their rival. It was the ultimate sign of respect for the man who is unquestionably the greatest center to ever play the game.

At seven feet, two inches tall, Kareem Abdul-Jabbar was born to be an NBA center. He had a four-year career at the University of California, Los Angeles (UCLA), where he led his team to win three NCAA titles. After college, the Milwaukee Bucks made Abdul-Jabbar the first overall pick in the 1969 NBA Draft. While it can take a few seasons for most college players to adjust to the NBA style of game, Abdul-Jabbar became an instant superstar. Dominating his opponents, he won the Rookie of the Year

Award and was named to the first of 19 All-Star teams. (When Abdul-Jabbar entered the league he was known by his birth name of Lew Alcindor. He changed his name the day after the Bucks won the 1971 NBA Championship.)

With such a commanding rookie season, fans wondered if Abdul-Jabbar would experience a sophomore slump. Surely, he couldn't top a season in which he averaged more than 28 points and 14 rebounds per game. They didn't have to wonder long. Abdul-Jabbar finished the 1970–71 NBA season by holding up both the NBA Finals trophy and the NBA Finals MVP Award. He led the league in scoring with 2,596 points, averaging 31.7 points per game, and earned his second straight All-Star appearance.

For Abdul-Jabbar, that was just the beginning. By the time he walked off the court for the final time in his career, Abdul-Jabbar had collected six NBA Championship titles, appeared in 19 All-Star Games, and had earned six league MVP Awards as well as two NBA Finals MVP Awards.

Abdul-Jabbar's career spanned 20 seasons, and although he is widely recognized as a Los Angeles Laker, it was during his first six seasons in the NBA, in Milwaukee, that he honed his game and built the foundation for greatness. He was an All-Star every season he played in Milwaukee. He was a fan favorite. And he perfected the "sky hook," considered by many analysts to be the greatest shot in basketball. When super-tall Abdul-Jabbar would launch himself up in the air to deliver a hook shot, it was practically unblockable by other, shorter players. It became his signature shot.

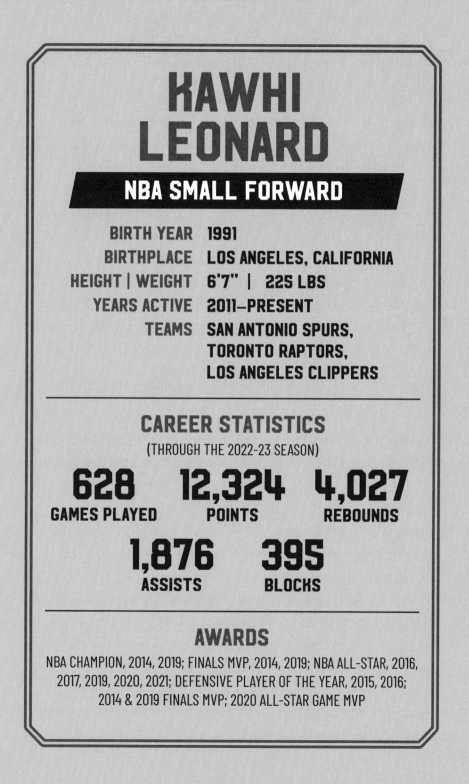

KAWHI LEONARD

NBA SMALL FORWARD

BIRTH YEAR	1991
BIRTHPLACE	LOS ANGELES, CALIFORNIA
HEIGHT | WEIGHT	6'7" | 225 LBS
YEARS ACTIVE	2011–PRESENT
TEAMS	SAN ANTONIO SPURS, TORONTO RAPTORS, LOS ANGELES CLIPPERS

CAREER STATISTICS

(THROUGH THE 2022-23 SEASON)

628
GAMES PLAYED

12,324
POINTS

4,027
REBOUNDS

1,876
ASSISTS

395
BLOCKS

AWARDS

NBA CHAMPION, 2014, 2019; FINALS MVP, 2014, 2019; NBA ALL-STAR, 2016, 2017, 2019, 2020, 2021; DEFENSIVE PLAYER OF THE YEAR, 2015, 2016; 2014 & 2019 FINALS MVP; 2020 ALL-STAR GAME MVP

HISTORY AT THE BUZZER

It was Game 7 of the 2019 NBA Eastern Conference Semifinals and the Toronto Raptors were locked in a fight with the Philadelphia 76ers. The winners would advance to the Eastern Conference Finals and for the losers, the season would be over. Kawhi Leonard had no intention of letting the 76ers celebrate on his home court. On this night, "The Klaw" wanted his second title.

With 4.2 seconds on the clock and the game tied at 90 points for each team, it looked as though the game was headed for overtime. The Raptors had one last chance to win—and they knew they had to get the ball into the hands of their superstar.

Just before the clock hit zero, Leonard launched a high-arcing shot over the outstretched arms of the opposing team's player. The ball bounced twice off one side of the rim, then twice more off the other side. It appeared to be moving in slow motion. Then, the ball gently fell through the hoop . . . and the Scotiabank Arena crowd erupted into applause.

Leonard ended the night with 41 points, leading his team even closer to an eventual NBA title. That thrilling moment cemented his place in history as one of the most clutch players in the game.

When the game is on the line, players want the ball in their hands—they'll want to take any last chance to score. Anyone who knows Kawhi Leonard—has played with him, coached him, or hung out with him—would say the same thing: *He wants the ball.*

Leonard has spent a lifetime overcoming challenges, managing heartbreak, and proving doubters wrong. On that cool May evening in Toronto, with nearly 20,000 fans screaming at the top of their lungs, Leonard did what Leonard has always done: He grabbed the ball and delivered.

A TOUGH CHILDHOOD

Kawhi Leonard learned early in life the importance of teamwork in overcoming adversity. Leonard is the youngest of five children, growing up with four older sisters. The challenge of five siblings coming together isn't much different from five distinct personalities coming together on the basketball court.

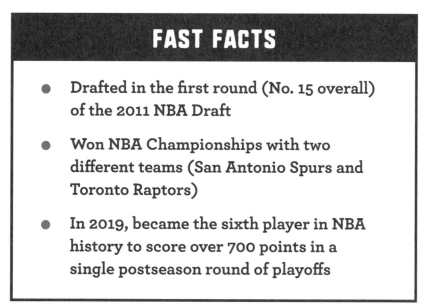

FAST FACTS

- **Drafted in the first round (No. 15 overall) of the 2011 NBA Draft**

- **Won NBA Championships with two different teams (San Antonio Spurs and Toronto Raptors)**

- **In 2019, became the sixth player in NBA history to score over 700 points in a single postseason round of playoffs**

Leonard started playing basketball early as a kid, growing up just outside of Los Angeles. Though his favorite sport was football, a passion he shared with his dad, Leonard developed early skills as a basketball player. Known for his larger-than-average hands and quiet demeanor on the court, Leonard left a powerful impression on his coaches. In a 2019 interview following Leonard's MVP performance in the NBA Finals, his former youth All-Star coach, David Williams, said, "He'd always challenge me. If you say anything was outstanding about him at that age, it was the fact that he played defense, and he enjoyed it."

As Leonard continued to grow and his skills improved, it soon became obvious to those around him that he was a special player who was destined for greatness. "When he showed up [at practice], I called my dad, and I said, 'You need to get down here right now,'" Leonard's high school coach, Tim Sweeney, recalled in a recent interview. "'I think we may have a future NBA player.'"

Sweeney got the opportunity to coach Leonard purely by chance. Leonard's mother was working on the day of his high school freshman tryouts, and he was unable to get a ride, so he missed them. When he spoke to the coach about a second chance, he was shown the door instead. It was a hard lesson to learn. After his freshman year, he transferred schools, and that was when he connected with Sweeney. That move would take his game to the next level.

By his junior year, Leonard was already thinking about a college scholarship. He was dominating on the basketball court. Off the court, he worked at his father's car wash in Compton, California. Scrubbing and polishing cars was tough, but Mark Leonard wanted his son to appreciate the importance of hard work. It is a trait Leonard carries with him to this day, as he is often the first in and last out of the gym.

Just when everything seemed picture-perfect for Leonard, tragedy struck: His father was killed. For Leonard, who was just 16 years old, it was devastating. He had lost his dad, his friend, and his mentor. Yet, Leonard did exactly what his dad taught him. He pressed on. The very next night he took to the court and scored 17 points.

From missing out on playing for his freshman team to losing his father, Leonard faced his childhood adversity head-on and poured all of his energy and drive into one thing: being the best basketball player on the court.

HARD WORK PAYS OFF

After attending three different high schools in four years, Leonard wasn't a highly recruited ballplayer. Though he had plenty of game tapes to prove his skills and the scouts were in the stands at almost every game he played, the offers weren't stacking up. In the end, Leonard decided to stay close to home and signed with San Diego State University.

Not exactly known as a basketball powerhouse, San Diego State boasted just four players who went on to play in the NBA, and there wasn't a single All-Star among them. But Leonard wasn't worried. His confidence in his skills was growing, and if San Diego State was where he would have to forge a path to the NBA, then so be it.

With an increasing number of players opting for just one year of college before declaring for the NBA draft, Leonard bucked the trend and spent two years at San Diego State. He led his team to compete back-to-back in the NCAA tournament, advancing as far as the "Sweet 16" during March Madness in his sophomore season. Leonard didn't put up the explosive offensive numbers of many first-round draft picks, but at San Diego State he displayed a balance to his game that drove his chances of a draft pick way up. He tied for a school record in his final season, averaging 15.5 points and 10.6 rebounds per game.

Those numbers were enough to make Leonard a first-round prospect, expected by analysts to go any-where between the 12th and 25th pick in the 2011 NBA Draft. So, it was no surprise when the Indiana Pacers selected Leonard with the 15th pick in the draft. What was a surprise was that within hours of drafting Leonard, the Pacers shipped him to San Antonio in exchange for a fellow first-round pick (from 2008), point guard George Hill.

For Leonard, the transition from San Diego State to San Antonio wasn't difficult. He played in 39 games during his rookie campaign, averaging just under eight points per game. His output, both offensively and defensively, would improve each year for the next several seasons as he got more comfortable with the pace and the power of NBA games.

Leonard advanced to the NBA Finals in just his second season in the league. Though the Spurs were beaten by the Miami Heat, they would return the following season for a rematch. In his second NBA Finals, Leonard shot an impressive career-high 29 points in a Game 3 win on the road in Miami, and got a personal best, scoring 20 or more points for three games straight. Following the game, Leonard reflected on his success: "Year after year I just kept getting more comfortable with the players on my team, and they started believing in me, and this year we won," he said. "I just believed in all the hard work I put in."

Unfortunately, Leonard's success with the Spurs took a stumble. By 2017, he had several injuries that limited his playing time. He played only nine games in the 2017–18 season. At one point, though the team's doctors cleared Leonard to play, he refused, opting to get a second opinion from his own medical professionals. Rumors spread that Leonard and his teammates were not getting along. A players-only meeting was held, and the message was clear: The players wanted Leonard back on the court and saw his absence as selfish. Leonard would never play another game for the Spurs. During the off-season, he sought a trade, and in April 2018, he got his wish: He was dealt to the Toronto Raptors.

Soon after the trade, the buzz began to build that Leonard had no interest in playing for them, and might even refuse to report to the team. Leonard had made it known that he preferred to be traded to his hometown team, the Los Angeles Lakers.

Leonard left after a single season as a Raptor, but not before playing electric basketball, setting career highs in points (26.6 per game) and rebounds (7.3 per game), and carrying the team on his back to its first NBA Championship.

As he held his second NBA Finals MVP trophy over his head, the fans, the media, and the basketball world knew Kawhi Leonard was headed to Los Angeles. On July 10, 2019, he signed a three-year, $103-million deal to join the Los Angeles Clippers.

Ten years after leaving Los Angeles in pursuit of a dream, Kawhi Leonard returned home wearing two NBA Championship rings and carrying two NBA Finals MVP trophies. Not bad for a kid who couldn't talk his way onto his freshman basketball squad!

HIS OWN DYNASTY

In professional sports, legacies are often formed. Leonard's legacy may be in his ability to easily move from team to team and still make those around him better.

Only three players in the history of the game have won the Finals MVP Award with two different teams: Kareem, LeBron, and Kawhi. Leonard won his first title and MVP Award with San Antonio and five years later duplicated the feat with Toronto. Most basketball experts believe it is only a matter of time before he adds Los Angeles to his list of title towns.

In a world where players measure their lives in online photos, Leonard chooses to be quieter. He doesn't use social media, avoids the celebrity side of the world he lives in, and peacefully goes about his business of being one of the most gifted men to ever play the game of basketball. That's a legacy worth leaving behind.

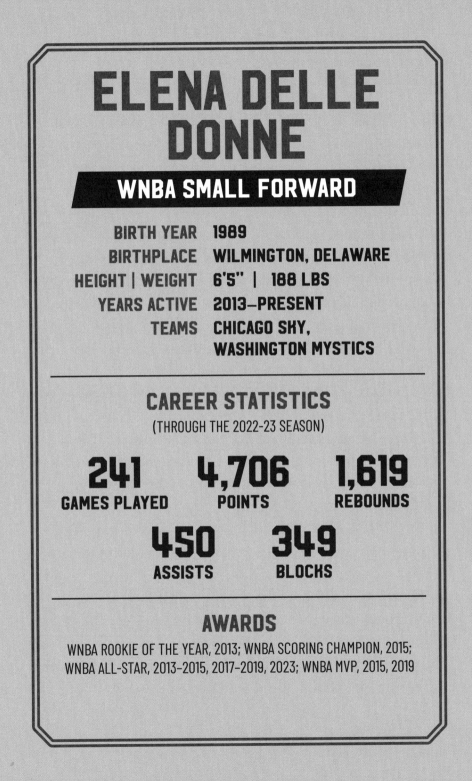

ELENA DELLE DONNE

WNBA SMALL FORWARD

BIRTH YEAR	1989
BIRTHPLACE	WILMINGTON, DELAWARE
HEIGHT | WEIGHT	6'5" | 188 LBS
YEARS ACTIVE	2013–PRESENT
TEAMS	CHICAGO SKY, WASHINGTON MYSTICS

CAREER STATISTICS

(THROUGH THE 2022-23 SEASON)

241
GAMES PLAYED

4,706
POINTS

1,619
REBOUNDS

450
ASSISTS

349
BLOCKS

AWARDS

WNBA ROOKIE OF THE YEAR, 2013; WNBA SCORING CHAMPION, 2015; WNBA ALL-STAR, 2013–2015, 2017–2019, 2023; WNBA MVP, 2015, 2019

FAMILY FIRST

The greatest story in the life of WNBA superstar Elena Delle Donne has nothing to do with her heroics on the hard court. Putting aside her domination during her four years playing basketball at the University of Delaware, her first-round selection in the 2013 WNBA Draft, her WNBA Championship title, her two league MVP Awards, and her Olympic gold medal—Delle Donne's legacy should be remembered not for what she did on the court, but for the reason she spends less time on it than virtually every WNBA star.

Delle Donne is the youngest of three children. Her oldest sister, Lizzie, was born blind and deaf and lives with cerebral palsy and autism. Lizzie has never seen her little sister play basketball, never heard her voice, and the two have never spoken—at least in the traditional sense. Yet Lizzie is the center of Delle Donne's world. Most WNBA stars play overseas in the off-season, earning millions of dollars to make up for the relatively low pay in the WNBA. Delle Donne has turned down every offer to play in Europe. Her reason is simple and pure: Family always comes first.

"Lizzie doesn't know that I play basketball," Delle Donne said during an interview for HBO's *Real Sports*. "She doesn't know that I'm six foot five. She just knows that I am one of her people and a really important person in her life . . . and that's all I want to be."

A modern athlete willing to completely cast aside any ego, not to mention millions of dollars in salary and endorsements in order to stay close to home with her family is remarkable, though Delle Donne doesn't see it that way. "I don't ever get cocky over basketball stuff. I can shoot a basketball. Who cares?" she said to ESPN in a 2019 interview shortly after she won her first WNBA title. "My sister has been dealt all these incredibly difficult cards, but still perseveres. She's always been my perspective."

OVERCOMING INJURY

Sometimes the biggest nights of a player's career don't show up on the stat sheets. For Delle Donne, Game 3 of the 2019 WNBA Finals was a career-defining game. Her Washington Mystics were tied 1–1 in the best of five

FAST FACTS

- Once made 59 consecutive free throws
- The most successful free-throw shooter (93.8%) in basketball history (for women and men)
- No. 2 overall pick in the 2013 WNBA Draft

games, and they were set to take on the Connecticut Sun next. Delle Donne had a monster Game 1, pouring in 22 points and getting her team the series-opening win. But a back injury forced her out early in Game 2, and, without her, the Sun destroyed the Mystics. The injury left fans wondering: Would their superstar return at all in the series? A postgame Magnetic Resonance Image (MRI) uncovered three herniated discs in her back. But Delle Donne wasn't going to let her team down.

Despite the serious back injury, she returned to the court for Game 3 and delivered a gritty performance. She seemed to struggle getting up and down the court, clearly hobbled by her bad back. Plus, she was wearing a face mask to protect her nose, which she had broken two weeks earlier—thanks to an elbow to the face. Despite her injuries, she got out 26 minutes of play time.

Her team managed a 14-point lead, and with just five minutes left in the game, the injured star was still on the court and delivering. Teammate Natasha Cloud lined up a jump shot from the point. The ball careened off the rim and Delle Donne managed to snatch the ball back from an offensive rebound and deliver a quick jump shot—expanding the lead to 16 points, and winning Game 3 for the Mystics. They also won Game 4.

Delle Donne saved her best for the deciding Game 5 of the series. Still hobbled by her injured back, she was determined to deliver the title to the home crowd at Entertainment and Sports Arena in the nation's capital. After helping her team to an 11-point lead, it was fitting that with 22 seconds left in the game, Delle Donne grabbed the game's final rebound and brought the ball up the court, keeping the opposing team from grabbing the ball and getting any points.

As she crossed midcourt, she let the ball drop to the floor, embracing her teammates as the final 10 seconds ran off the clock. She had done it: The Mystics were the 2019 champions of the WNBA!

HOME IN DELAWARE

Elena Delle Donne's six-foot-five frame, built for power basketball, was something she inherited from her parents. Her dad, Ernie, is six feet six and a former Division I basketball player, and her mom, Joan, is six feet two. At home in Delaware, in addition to her sister Lizzie, she also has an older brother, Gene. Delle Donne has said that playing with and competing against Gene and other boys was a big part of her development as an athlete. "I could do whatever I wanted as a girl, whatever my brother did," she says on her official website. "I could play against the boys and achieve whatever they did."

Delle Donne first began playing basketball, or at least playing *with* a basketball, when she was four years old. As her height exploded, so too did the natural expectations that Delle Donne would follow in her father's footsteps and play basketball. She loved the game as a child and towering over most of her classmates gave her a distinct edge. But it wasn't an edge Delle Donne always liked. Standing out as a girl who is six feet tall in the eighth grade comes with plenty of disadvantages. In an in-depth profile for *ESPN The Magazine* in 2016, Delle Donne talked about being seen as a "monster" because of her height. She also reflects that she felt pressured by her height to play either basketball or volleyball. "With a woman, there's a general sense that she has to play basketball because what else is she going to do?" Delle Donne told the magazine.

Despite her mixed feelings, she played both sports and excelled as an athlete. Elite athletes often receive college scholarship offers by their junior year in high school. Delle Donne received her first offer to play college ball on a scholarship when she was in middle school!

The teenager continued to develop her already rare talent on the court at Ursuline Academy, a private Catholic school near her family's home in Delaware. In four years at Ursuline, Delle Donne led the team to three state championships and earned an offer to play college ball for one of the strongest women's basketball programs in the nation: the University of Connecticut (UConn) Huskies.

After initially accepting the offer to play for the Huskies, Delle Donne backed out and opted to stay close to home, instead joining the University of Delaware. It wasn't UConn, but it was the place where Delle Donne would fine-tune her game and earn an eventual second overall pick in the 2013 WNBA Draft.

FINALLY, A CHAMPION

While at Delaware, she led the program to 104 wins and an appearance in the 2013 "Sweet 16" tournament. After such amazing success, it was time for Delle Donne to take her game to the next level. The Chicago Sky held the second pick in the 2013 WNBA Draft, and they saw her as the future face of their franchise. She wasted no time in proving they made the right choice.

In the 2013 season opening game, Delle Donne lit up the scoreboard with 22 points as she led the Sky to a win against the Phoenix Mercury and Brittney Griner, the player chosen ahead of her in the draft. Her first game was just a taste of what was to come. Delle Donne went on to have a stunning rookie season. She averaged more than 18 points per game in over 30 contests. She also became an instant fan favorite, leading the entire NBA in All-Star voting and being named the WNBA Rookie of the Year.

After reaching the playoffs in her first season, expectations were high for Delle Donne and the Sky in 2014. Unfortunately, illness caused her to miss more than half of the season. Six years earlier, in 2008, Delle Donne had been bitten by a tick and contracted Lyme disease. Symptoms of the disease often can resurface many months or even years later. The chronic condition flared up in 2014 and forced her to sit out a long stretch of games.

The next year, fully recovered from the illness that sidelined her in 2014, Delle Donne had her most exciting season yet. She was unstoppable on the offensive side of the ball, leading the league in scoring with more than 23 points per game as she helped the Sky finish with a 21–13 record. Delle Donne earned another All-Star Game appearance, a scoring title, and her first League MVP Award to cap the best season of her professional career so far!

In her four seasons in Chicago, the Sky made the post-season playoffs three times. But even with Delle Donne's outstanding performance, they were never able to win a title. When she was traded to the Washington Mystics prior to the 2017 WNBA season, her chances seemed to decrease even further. The Mystics had never won the WNBA crown and had finished the previous season with a 13–21 record. Still, Delle Donne was determined. It took three seasons in Washington, but as she promised when she arrived, Delle Donne delivered the WNBA Championship in a five-game, thrilling series against the Connecticut Sun.

For a player who suffered numerous setbacks over her career, winning the WNBA Championship was the culmination of years of blood, sweat, and tears.

FIGHTING FOR OTHERS

Though still in her prime, Delle Donne has already established a deep, multilayered legacy thanks to her on-court accomplishments: WNBA Champion, league MVP, consistent All-Star, and one of the most dominant women to ever play the game. But, as with her unselfish love for her sister, Lizzie, Delle Donne's biggest legacy may endure off the court.

In 2017, Delle Donne married her longtime girlfriend, Amanda Clifton. She shared the engagement with the world a year earlier in an article in *Vogue* magazine. It was her first public acknowledgment that she was gay, and for young people who looked up to the WNBA star, it was encouraging and inspiring. Since her announcement, Delle Donne has used her celebrity status to advocate for LGBTQIA+ issues and to fight for equality for all.

She also launched the Elena Delle Donne Charitable Foundation, a nonprofit dedicated to supporting two causes close to her heart: people with special needs and research for Lyme disease. She further supports the efforts of special needs athletes by running the Delle Donne Skills Academy basketball camp, where able-bodied players compete alongside players with disabilities. "There's no greater feeling than getting to spend time with them and see them work with one another, and the joy of sport," she said in a 2018 interview.

Perhaps Delle Donne's biggest impact is her determination to show that female athletes are every bit as valuable as their male counterparts—and that their value extends well beyond their playing careers. "Women aren't valued the same way men are in the workforce," she said during a 2018 television appearance. "It gets frustrating, but you've just got to continue to fight the battle."

Fans may see Elena Delle Donne as one of the greatest to ever play the game of basketball. She is much more than that. She is a role model, advocate, author, speaker, and champion for women. Above all, she is someone who has refused to be identified solely by her athletic success, instead identifying basketball not as who she is, but as an important part of the person she has become.

Honorable Mentions SMALL FORWARD

JIMMY BUTLER

Jimmy Butler is something of an anomaly: He is one of the best small forwards in the game, yet Butler has played for four NBA teams since 2017. Originally drafted by the Chicago Bulls in 2011, Butler was traded away to the Minnesota Timberwolves and has since spent one season with the Philadelphia 76ers before joining the Miami Heat.

He averaged more than 20 points per game in five of his first eight seasons, earning four trips to the All-Star Game. Butler has seen his productivity drop as he has bounced from team to team, but he earns a spot on this list for one reason: He is a winner. He has appeared in the playoffs every season he has been in the league.

As much as he loves the game and as talented as he is on the floor, Butler sees himself as more than just a basketball player. "Life isn't always about basketball," he said during an interview shortly after signing with the Miami Heat. "It's about principle. It's about character. It's about so many different things."

In an era where so many athletes are consumed with fame and fortune, Butler has managed to deliver on the court and stay balanced off it.

KLAY THOMPSON

It can be easy for a player to get lost in the crowd of talent playing for the Golden State Warriors. Klay Thompson has spent much of his career in the shadows of Steph Curry, Kevin Durant, and Draymond Green. Still, Thompson has proven himself to be one of the best three-point shooters in the league and as clutch a player as anyone in the game today.

Thompson's three-point game is unquestioned, but on an early-season Monday in 2018, he took it to the next level. Thompson and the Warriors were in Chicago to take on the Bulls, and Thompson had the drive. That night, he set an NBA record with 14 three-pointers in the game, finishing with 52 points. And he didn't even play in the fourth quarter!

But that was the second NBA record Thompson earned while showcasing his scoring skills. The first came in 2015, when he set a record for most points scored in a quarter. He lit up the Sacramento Kings for 37 points in the third quarter of his team's 126–101 win.

Thompson's stellar offensive skills plus his popularity as a teammate combined to earn him a five-year, $190 million "max contract" from Golden State in the summer of 2019. But two devastating injuries—ACL and torn achilles—kept Klay from making good on that contract. On January 9, 2022, after 941 days in street clothes, Klay suited up with a vengeance in a win against Cleveland: 17 points (including 3 three-pointers), 3 rebounds, an assist, and a steal in just 20 total minutes on the floor. Needless to say, Warriors fans were ecstatic!

MAYA MOORE

Maya Moore was a standout at the basketball powerhouse University of Connecticut before being selected by the Minnesota Lynx with the first overall pick in the 2011 WNBA Draft. Since then, Moore has done nothing but prove how impressive she is. In her first eight seasons, Moore has collected four WNBA titles and a pair of Olympic Gold Medals. She has also succeeded playing on teams overseas.

In a 2018 interview with *Slam* magazine, Moore offered some advice to fans who wonder what it takes to reach the level of success she has enjoyed in her professional career. "To do anything great, you have to have a passion for what you're doing," she said. "You definitely have to have meaning in what you're doing and finding purpose in what you're doing. As long as I feel like I'm doing what I'm being called to do, then I know I'm where I'm supposed to be."

Moore's passion for the game was never more evident than in Game 3 of the 2015 WNBA Finals. Her Lynx were tied 77–77 with the Indiana Fever. With just 1.4 seconds left in the game, Moore caught a pass. She then smartly avoided the defender, went airborne, and buried the game-winning three-pointer at the buzzer! The Lynx went on to win the third of Moore's four championship titles. She retired in 2023.

Legendary Great SMALL FORWARD

LARRY BIRD

It would be impossible to single out a greatest moment, or perhaps even a greatest game, in the Hall of Fame career of Boston Celtics legend Larry Bird. But if pressed, a case could be made for what happened on May 13, 1984. The Celtics were deadlocked 3–3 versus the New York Knicks in the Eastern Conference Semifinals. Larry Bird took the home court, looking to clinch Game 7 and advance his team to face the Milwaukee Bucks.

The Celtics won the opening tip-off and Bird wasted no time making his presence felt. Catching a pass, Bird executed a flawless jump shot for the first points of the game. From then on, "Larry Legend," as he was nicknamed, went on to win one of the most commanding games of his career. Bird managed 39 points, sending the Knicks packing and moving his Celtics closer to winning the NBA Championship title. It was the second of the three titles Bird would win in his 13-year career, all spent with the Celtics.

Bird was known for his toughness on the court and his ability to make stunt-like shots that seemed impossible. Bird accomplished something that only two other basketball greats (Wilt Chamberlain and Bill Russell) have achieved: He won the NBA MVP Award for three consecutive seasons (1984–86).

Bird was the centerpiece of the Celtics dynasty of the 1980s, alongside Robert Parish, Kevin McHale, and Dennis Johnson. Together, they collected three championship rings. But it was a cross-country rivalry that made for one of the most compelling aspects of Bird's career. In the 1980s, the Boston Celtics and Los Angeles Lakers were two of the NBA's biggest rivals. As the stars of each team, Larry Bird and Magic Johnson were the faces of that rivalry.

They would later appear in television commercials together, selling everything from hamburgers to sneakers, and speak of each other warmly as friends. But at the peak of the rivalry, they were fierce competitors. Bird versus Johnson was must-see TV, anytime the Celtics and Lakers matched up.

Bird's career was cut short by a recurring back injury that required multiple surgeries. But before he called it quits, Larry Legend earned 12 All-Star appearances to go along with his three NBA titles and three MVP awards. He was also a member of the historic 1992 US Olympic basketball team, dubbed the "Dream Team." Playing alongside Magic Johnson and Michael Jordan, Bird collected a gold medal as the Americans swept through the Olympics.

In 1998, Bird was elected to the Naismith Memorial Basketball Hall of Fame. His jersey number 33 was retired and hangs from the rafters in Boston. In a city that was home to such sports legends as Ted Williams, Babe Ruth, Bobby Orr, Bill Russell, and Tom Brady, Larry Bird remains one of the most accomplished—and most popular—athletes to ever represent Boston.

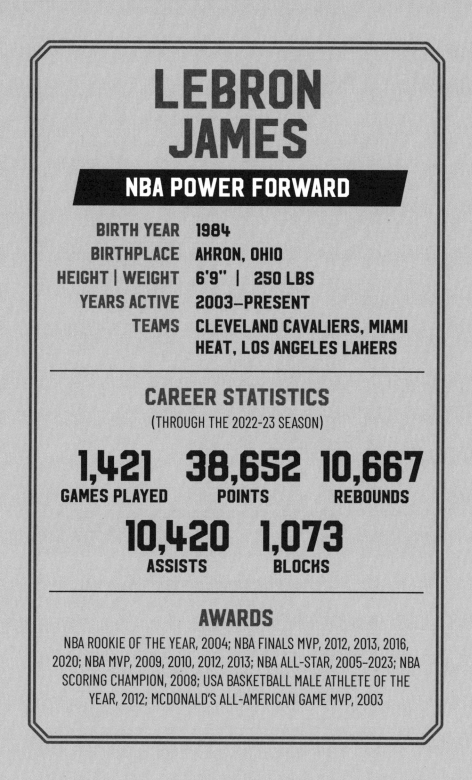

LEBRON JAMES

NBA POWER FORWARD

BIRTH YEAR	**1984**
BIRTHPLACE	**AKRON, OHIO**
**HEIGHT	WEIGHT**	**6'9"	250 LBS**
YEARS ACTIVE	**2003–PRESENT**
TEAMS	**CLEVELAND CAVALIERS, MIAMI HEAT, LOS ANGELES LAKERS**

CAREER STATISTICS
(THROUGH THE 2022-23 SEASON)

1,421
GAMES PLAYED

38,652
POINTS

10,667
REBOUNDS

10,420
ASSISTS

1,073
BLOCKS

AWARDS
NBA ROOKIE OF THE YEAR, 2004; NBA FINALS MVP, 2012, 2013, 2016, 2020; NBA MVP, 2009, 2010, 2012, 2013; NBA ALL-STAR, 2005–2023; NBA SCORING CHAMPION, 2008; USA BASKETBALL MALE ATHLETE OF THE YEAR, 2012; MCDONALD'S ALL-AMERICAN GAME MVP, 2003

TRULY A KING

Is LeBron James the best active NBA player in his position right now? He has been the greatest, without doubt, but now his body has 20 NBA seasons of wear and tear on it. Even so, James is still starting, still averaging nearly 30 points per game, and still fighting to win the NBA title with his third team. Whether he is playing for Cleveland, Miami, or Los Angeles, LeBron James has been making an incredible impact on the game since he was 18 years old.

Like golf's Tiger Woods, James is the athlete with the rare ability to make people who aren't even fans of the game tune in and watch. His talent on the court, his charisma, and his leadership are legendary. Fans (and non-fans) know that every time James takes the court, history may be made. For instance, take the night in

FAST FACTS

- **No. 1 overall pick in the 2003 NBA Draft**

- **19-time All-Star**

- **Averaged at least 25 points, 5 rebounds, and 5 assists per game in 15 seasons (most of any player in history)**

2019 when James set an NBA record as the first player to record a triple-double (a score of at least ten or more in three of the main statistical categories, like points, assists, rebounds, etc.) against every team in the league. Or the night in 2014 when he poured in a career-high 61 points against the Charlotte Bobcats.

James is special. He is more than just a talent on the basketball court—he has defined a generation. He may be not only the greatest to ever play the game—but also the greatest that ever *will* play the game. He is, as a newspaper first dubbed him while in high school, "King James."

CARRYING HIS TEAM

In Game 7 of the 2013 NBA Finals, the Miami Heat were looking to win back-to-back titles. They were at home, taking on the San Antonio Spurs to close out what had been a brutal, hard-fought series. Game 7 would be no different. It was back and forth all night, and with less than a minute left, the Heat held on to a two-point lead. James has already had a monster night, with 33 points and a dozen rebounds. But when his team needed him most, when the series and the title were on the line, the King delivered.

After Tim Duncan of the Spurs missed an easy game-tying basket, the Heat brought the ball up the court. The sold-out crowd on their feet in the Miami arena had little doubt about who was going to get the ball. Just after the time-out, James caught an inbounds pass, then appeared to be ready to move to the hoop. Instead he suddenly pulled up, creating space between himself and the defenders, and executed a jump shot that gave the Heat a two-possession lead with less than 30 seconds to go!

The Spurs had one last chance to make a foul on the other team and then hope to get the ball in their possession. They chose to send James back to the line to shoot for the Heat with their season hanging in the balance. James coolly stepped up and buried both free throws, along with the Spurs' season. James had put the Heat on his back and carried them to their second NBA Championship title!

He finished the game with 37 points, 12 boards, 4 assists, and a pair of steals. He was a perfect five-for-five from three-point range and eight-for-eight from the free-throw line. Dominant players—true superstars—always want the ball when the game is on the line. James is no different. When it matters most, King James takes control and delivers the clutch shots that lead his team to the title.

FROM POVERTY TO RICHES

James was born in Akron, Ohio, in 1984. His mother was just 16 years old and his father wasn't in the picture. James grew up poor. His mother bounced around jobs and that meant James lived his childhood on the move.

He and his mom moved from apartment to apartment, packing up when they could no longer pay the rent. He slept on friends' couches, switched schools frequently, and struggled to fit in. One year he missed more than 100 days of school. For young James, his days weren't spent visualizing a career in the NBA—they were spent surviving.

During those early years, basketball wasn't even a possibility. His sports interest began with football. A coach had seen him race some friends in a parking lot and recognized that his speed was special. At nine years old, James played running back for an under-10 youth football team in Akron. His athletic gifts were immediately noticeable: His size and speed made him impossible to tackle.

When James did begin to play basketball, it began with a milk crate nailed to a telephone pole, forming a crude basket. Who could have ever imagined that the poor kid from Akron shooting a ball through a milk crate would one day grow up to be an NBA superstar?

By middle school, LeBron was already dunking the basketball, and as a freshman at St. Vincent-St. Mary High School, he was already receiving national attention from scouts and the media. James had earned the hype. He led his team to a perfect 27–0 record as a freshman, winning the state championship. Later, as a junior, James was featured on the cover of *Sports Illustrated*—a first in the history of the magazine. Under a picture of James, the headline referred to him as "The Chosen One."

The NBA now has a rule barring teams from drafting players straight from high school. But this rule didn't exist in 2003. Thus, the Cleveland Cavaliers used the first overall selection in the 2003 NBA Draft to select St. Vincent-St. Mary forward LeBron James. The kid who grew up in poverty in Akron was now a millionaire in Cleveland.

THE DAY IT BEGAN

After years of anticipation and more hype than had ever been afforded a high school athlete in any sport, LeBron James took the court on the road against the Sacramento Kings on October 29, 2003. The world watched and wondered how the teenager the media called "The Chosen One" would respond in his first regular season NBA game.

Less than two minutes into his first game, James went hard to the basket and pulled down a defensive rebound. He glided up the court before delivering a beautiful alley-oop pass to his teammate, who then managed a slam dunk. James would finish his first professional game leading his team in points (25), assists (9), and steals (4).

James later gave an interview during his rookie season where he explained how he handled his new life in the NBA. "There's no pressure for me, because I'm doing something I love to do, that's play the game of basketball," he said. His rookie campaign of 2003–04 posted seven games with 30 or more points. He appeared in all 82 games for the Cavs. He was a runaway choice for the Rookie of the Year Award. And for the first time in a long time, fans in Cleveland had something to be excited about.

His first taste of the postseason came in a first-round matchup against the Washington Wizards. In the pivotal Game 5 of the series, James delivered a performance that still ranks among the best of his career. From the moment he won the opening tip-off, James used his size and strength to manhandle the Wizards' defenders. Time and again he pulled up to shoot finesse jump shots over the outstretched arms of the defenders.

But James saved his best for last. Trailing 120–119 with just 3.6 seconds left in the game, James took the inbounds pass from Larry Hughes. Many players would have panicked and thrown up the quick shot. Not James. He deftly weaved through the defense and calmly laid the ball up and in for the game winner. The Cavaliers went on to win the series and the legacy of James in the post-season was born.

G.O.A.T.

When he eventually walks away from the game, James will leave basketball as the greatest basketball player of all time. Sure, many will point to Michael Jordan's achievements, but that's where the details of LeBron's career, his legacy, and his place in history as the G.O.A.T. (Greatest of All Time) dominate.

Consider this: Michael Jordan won six titles, but he did it with a single dynasty team—the Chicago Bulls. LeBron has shown the ability to win championships with multiple teams. LeBron has already topped MJ in every major statistical category—including points, rebounds, assists, and blocks. He has more All-Star appearances and he even tops Jordan in Olympic medals, 3 to 2. In 2023, he became the all-time leading scorer, passing Kareem Abdul-Jabaar.

Fans will argue that Jordan stepped away from the game for four seasons in two separate retirements and, had he played, he would have had the numbers to top LeBron. But the fact that James has performed at the highest level for so many years, without a break, simply adds to King James's legacy. Straight from high school, he stepped into the NBA and transformed the entire league.

James has strengthened his legacy off the court, too. His philanthropy through the LeBron James Family Foundation includes founding an elementary school in his hometown of Akron to serve disadvantaged youth. Through his foundation, he also pledged to spend more than $41 million to pay for 1,100 Akron students to attend college for free. His charitable work has earned him many accolades, including the NBA Citizenship Award.

James is also an accomplished businessman. His estimated income in 2019 was $89 million, with almost two thirds of that cash coming from his business ventures and endorsements. Wealth doesn't make a legacy, but what a person does with that wealth certainly does; James has chosen to use his fame and fortune to contribute millions of dollars to help young people excel, to create jobs, and to create generational security for his family.

Years from now, as historians reflect on the game of basketball, the legacy of LeBron James will be summed up in seven simple words: the greatest that ever played the game.

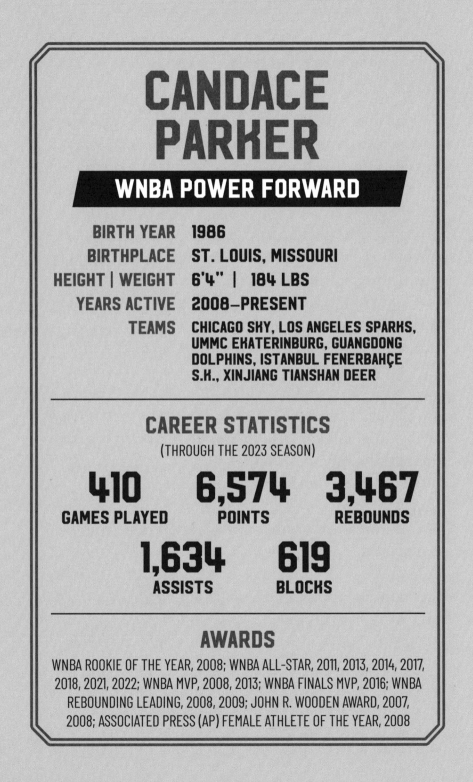

CANDACE PARKER

WNBA POWER FORWARD

BIRTH YEAR	**1986**
BIRTHPLACE	**ST. LOUIS, MISSOURI**
HEIGHT | WEIGHT	**6'4" | 184 LBS**
YEARS ACTIVE	**2008–PRESENT**
TEAMS	**CHICAGO SKY, LOS ANGELES SPARKS, UMMC EKATERINBURG, GUANGDONG DOLPHINS, ISTANBUL FENERBAHÇE S.K., XINJIANG TIANSHAN DEER**

CAREER STATISTICS
(THROUGH THE 2023 SEASON)

410
GAMES PLAYED

6,574
POINTS

3,467
REBOUNDS

1,634
ASSISTS

619
BLOCKS

AWARDS

WNBA ROOKIE OF THE YEAR, 2008; WNBA ALL-STAR, 2011, 2013, 2014, 2017, 2018, 2021, 2022; WNBA MVP, 2008, 2013; WNBA FINALS MVP, 2016; WNBA REBOUNDING LEADING, 2008, 2009; JOHN R. WOODEN AWARD, 2007, 2008; ASSOCIATED PRESS (AP) FEMALE ATHLETE OF THE YEAR, 2008

RISING ABOVE ADVERSITY

Basketball is a physical game, and players usually use the off-season to rest their bodies and minds and to recover for the season ahead. For Candace Parker, however, there is no off-season. Like all WNBA players, Parker's salary isn't what you might expect for a professional athlete. While top NBA players earn more than $50 million per season, the average WNBA salary is just over $113,000 a year. To supplement her WNBA salary, Parker travels overseas, playing in Russia, Turkey, and China. Between her WNBA career, her overseas career, and two trips to the Olympics, Parker has never experienced a true off-season. Without that built-in off-season, WNBA players like Parker are prone to more injuries. Though she is only in her mid-thirties, her body has endured a double-digit number of surgeries and grueling rehabilitations just to stay on the court.

Off the court, Parker has faced the negativity that comes with being a six-foot-four female basketball player. She has faced sexism, racism, and taunts that her professional team couldn't beat most high school boys' teams. Though she tries to channel the adversity to fuel her on the court, she isn't immune to the hurt, especially when it comes to issues of race.

"Racism has been an issue in our country for a very long time, but women's suffrage has been here an even longer time," she said during a WNBA roundtable discussion with some of the league's top players. "So, with that

FAST FACTS

- No. 1 overall pick in the 2008 WNBA Draft

- First player to earn WNBA MVP and Rookie of the Year in the same season

- First woman to dunk in an NCAA tournament game

combination, being Black *and* a woman, you know . . ." She doesn't bother to finish the sentence because every woman at the table *does* know. Still, Parker is proud of her career and all that she has accomplished on the court. She is proud to be a role model for her daughter. And she is proud to have overcome so much, battled so hard, and still play the game she loves.

"You know, there's obstacles in life, and it's about how you handle it," she said in an interview prior to the start of the 2016 season. "Sometimes it's not what happens, but rather your reaction to it."

A HISTORIC DUNK

First-round NCAA tournament games don't often generate much national buzz. Such was the case in 2006, when the University of Tennessee Lady Volunteers (Lady Vols) took on the Army Black Knights in the opening round of the tournament. Tennessee was expected to easily top Army in the game, which they did, 102–54. But a moment within that victory made real history.

Early in the first half, with the Lady Vols holding a two-point lead, Tennessee's Sidney Spencer grabbed a loose ball and tossed a long pass downcourt to Parker. The freshman raced toward the basket with one defender trailing her. Parker drove to the hoop, leaped in the air, and delivered a one-handed dunk! It may have been worth only two points, but it was a historic basket—Parker became the first woman in the history of the NCAA tournament to dunk a ball. Later, in the second half, her team comfortably out in front by 31 points, Parker delivered her second dunk of the game.

Parker prides herself on being a well-rounded basketball player when it comes to her skills. She has resisted being too closely linked to her ability to dunk the basketball. Following her history-making effort against Army, Parker was quick to downplay the achievement. "I've only dunked in one game. I don't want that to be my identity," she said at the time. "I want to be known for an all-around game."

The reality is, in a sport where very few women dunk, Parker's ability to do so has earned her accolades. In more than 100 years, no woman had ever accomplished what Parker did that night in Cleveland. And in the 23-year history of the WNBA, only seven players have dunked in a game, including Parker. By the time she threw down her first WNBA dunk, the magnitude of the NCAA milestone had changed for Parker, and she seemed more willing to embrace her role as a power player. "I was really excited to do it in front of the Los Angeles Sparks fans," she said in an interview following the game.

Parker sees herself as paving the way for girls to follow in her footsteps the way she followed in those of Lisa Leslie, her Sparks teammate and the first WNBA player to dunk in league history. "Lisa was the first generation, I'm the next generation," she said. "Then there's gonna be somebody out here doing windmills, it's just a matter of time."

INSPIRED BY BROTHERS

Candace Parker grew up in Naperville, Illinois, near Chicago. That meant she was a Chicago Bulls fan. It was the height of Michael Jordan's career and Parker was exposed to a lot of basketball growing up. In addition to watching Jordan, Scottie Pippen, and Dennis Rodman perform for the Bulls, Parker watched her older brothers, Anthony and Marcus. Both were serious basketball players and Parker would often accompany them to the park with their dad, Larry, while they played.

Despite this early exposure and love for the game, Parker didn't have any plans to play basketball herself. She was a soccer player as a kid. But as Parker was preparing to head to high school, things changed. Encouraged by her father and inspired by her brothers, she decided to take up basketball competitively. "I always wanted to do everything they did," she said of her brothers. "They're so much older than me, so we never really played against each other. I just really did everything they did and wanted to emulate their game."

With her height, natural athletic ability, and competitive nature, Parker soon excelled at basketball. In high school, Parker was an instant superstar. Her high school coach, Andrew Nussbaum, shared a story with *USA Today* in 2018 recounting the night Parker dunked the ball for the first time in a high school game. "She got it on the break, and you could tell that she was gonna try again," he said. "Then she just threw it down. It wasn't a home game, and there were a lot of people there, but I think everyone was just shocked. It was pretty incredible."

Nussbaum shared another side of Parker in that interview, one that speaks to her character. "She loved to fill the water cups for her teammates when she wasn't playing. She's probably the best high school girl's player to ever play the game, and here she is doubling as the water girl," he said. "She also used to look at the scorebook to see who hadn't scored yet, so she could get them the ball."

After graduation, Parker used her high school achievements to earn a scholarship to play Division I ball at the University of Tennessee under legendary coach Pat Summit. In college, Parker was a force for the Lady Vols, leading the team to back-to-back national championships. Instead of playing in her senior season, Parker turned her sights toward the 2008 Summer Olympics in Beijing, China, followed by a career in professional basketball.

In April 2008, Parker was taken by the Los Angeles Sparks with the first overall pick in the WNBA draft. Four months later, she reached her other goal, winning the gold medal as part of Team USA!

A LONG-AWAITED TROPHY

Parker's WNBA run kicked off with a road game against the Phoenix Mercury, and the rookie shined from the opening tip-off. She finished the first game of her professional career with a team high of 34 points as her Sparks topped the Mercury, 99–94. Parker finished her rookie campaign averaging 18.5 points per game and 9.5 boards. The 22-year-old became the first player in WNBA history to win both the Rookie of the Year Award and the league MVP Award in the same season.

Despite Parker's continued stellar performance, the Sparks fell short of the championship year after year. The team hadn't taken home a championship trophy since 2003. Finally, in 2016, the Sparks broke through. It was the first and only season of her career that Parker started every game. She led the Sparks to a 26–8 record in the regular season, but it was the postseason playoffs that mattered.

Analysts felt like this was the best Sparks team of Parker's tenure. However, they didn't win their division, instead finishing second to the Minnesota Lynx and entering the postseason as the number two seed.

Could Parker lead an upset and overcome their rivals for the title?

After a quiet first two games in the series, Parker exploded in Game 3 with 24 points, leading the Sparks to a crucial home win and a 2–1 series lead. The Lynx took Game 4, setting up a dramatic finale for the WNBA Championship.

With the season and the title on the line, Parker was incredible. She collected 12 rebounds in the game along with scoring 28 points, none more important than her final basket. Trailing 74–73 with 23 seconds left in the road game, the Sparks needed a bucket. Parker delivered, grabbing a feed from teammate Nneka Ogwumike, and banking a shot off the glass of the backboard for the lead. Two possessions later, the Sparks were the WNBA Champions and Parker was named the series MVP!

FIGHT FOR GENDER EQUALITY

Parker is outspoken that there ought to be equality and a sense of oneness among professional basketball players on both sides of the gender line. (It is worth noting that Parker was married to former NBA player Shelden Williams and her brother is former NBA player Anthony Parker.)

In a league where many of the players hold basketball camps and other events aimed at working with young girls, Parker pursues a different direction. Her basketball programs include boys *and* girls learning the game side by side. "I think it's just as important for guys and girls to understand that leaders can come in different shapes, sizes, backgrounds, whatever," Parker said in 2019. "And you can't just preach to girls, because that's not going to create change."

Perhaps her legacy will be defined by the "what ifs" of her career. What if Parker hadn't endured seven knee surgeries? What if she hadn't dislocated her shoulder in 2010 during a game? Injuries are part of professional sports, but Parker seems to have had more than her fair share. What if she had been able to stay healthier—would there be more titles?

After she retires, time will tell how Parker's legacy is viewed on the court. But like many WNBA players, she will be remembered for her pioneering efforts off the court to advance the game of women's basketball. Players and fans of the WNBA have long been outspoken about the need for higher player salaries. Parker has been among those voices.

Honorable Mentions POWER FORWARD

GIANNIS ANTETOKOUNMPO

The man they call "the Greek Freak" has put the Milwaukee Bucks back on the map as a legitimate NBA powerhouse. Giannis Antetokounmpo took an unusual route to the NBA. Born in Greece to Nigerian parents, Antetokounmpo didn't even begin playing basketball until he was a teenager. When he eventually joined a youth team in Greece, he walked four miles each way to practice and often slept in the gym afterward.

In 2013, Antetokounmpo became eligible for the NBA draft and the Milwaukee Bucks selected the 18-year-old as the 15th pick. Since then, he has improved every year he's been in the league, posting remarkable numbers the last three seasons and earning three consecutive trips to the All-Star Game.

In 2019, he posted career highs with 30.5 points and 12.9 rebounds per game, capturing his first NBA MVP Award. His rise has coincided with the success of the Bucks. The team made the playoffs in each of Antetokounmpo's All-Star years, and in 2021, they finally won the NBA Finals.

BLAKE GRIFFIN

Blake Griffin's career has been complicated. Drafted in 2009 by the Los Angeles Clippers with the first overall pick, Griffin missed his entire first season due to injury. He bounced back in 2010–11, capturing the Rookie of the Year Award and earning the first of five consecutive All-Star nods. Then the injuries returned. Griffin missed big parts of the next three seasons battling foot, shoulder, and hand injuries. Despite posting strong numbers even during his injury-filled seasons, the Clippers had seen enough. In the 2017–18 season, the Clippers traded away their former top pick to the Detroit Pistons. But Griffin wasn't done.

In his first season as a Piston, the six-foot-nine, 250-pound man delivered a career high in points, averaging 24.5 in 75 games. He returned to his pre-injury form and on October 23, 2018, delivered a performance reminiscent of his early years in Los Angeles. Taking on the Philadelphia 76ers at home, Griffin had a monster game. He poured in a career-high 50 points, scoring from all over the floor. But it was in overtime that Griffin delivered his best basketball.

With the Pistons trailing 132–130 and five seconds to go, Detroit was down to its last shot. Griffin took the inbounds pass, drove the lane, and laid in the basket to tie the game with 1.8 seconds on the clock! But he wasn't done. Griffin drew the foul on the play and stepped to the line with a chance to win the game. Griffin coolly knocked down the game winner, capping the best offensive night of his NBA career!

TINA CHARLES

Over the last decade, Tina Charles has proven to be one of the most reliable and consistent players in the WNBA. Charles was drafted by the Connecticut Sun in 2010 and didn't miss any stretch of time due to injury until 2022. She has averaged more than 18 points and nearly 10 rebounds per game and has been named a perennial All-Star, making eight appearances in her 14 seasons.

In six trips to the postseason, Charles has been the player her teams have leaned on to deliver big games. Her deepest playoff run came in 2015 with the New York Liberty. Charles put up 122 points in the Liberty's two playoff series. Unfortunately, Charles has never led her team to a WNBA Championship title. But the

2012 WNBA MVP dominated for a decade and the lack of championship rings doesn't diminish that. She holds the record for the fastest player to reach 50 career double-doubles, doing it in her first 75 WNBA games. She led the league in scoring in 2016 and she is an elite two-way player, having led the league in rebounding in four seasons. Charles is still in her prime, and whether the titles come or not, she is clearly an elite power forward in the WNBA.

Legendary Great POWER FORWARD

TIM DUNCAN

Players are often judged by how they perform in clutch situations. With the game on the line, with one shot to win, do they deliver? In his prime, no player in the NBA was better at buzzer-beating clutch shots than San Antonio Spurs power forward Tim Duncan.

But Duncan was more than just a clutch player. He was as complete a basketball player as the game has seen. On offense, he delivered countless buzzer beaters and crucial baskets. He posted a career average of 19 points per game over 19 seasons in his 19-year career for the Spurs. But he was equally skilled at defense. His play earned him All-Defensive First Team honors eight times. And if players are ultimately measured by how much they win, Duncan delivered. When he retired in 2016, Duncan was only the third player in league history to win 1,000 games. Duncan raised the NBA Championship trophy five times for the Spurs while becoming the only player in the history of the NBA to win a title in three different decades.

In addition to his five championship rings, Duncan's trophy case is crowded with the accolades befitting one of the greatest players to ever step onto an NBA court. He was named MVP of three of the five finals he won. Duncan was twice named league MVP, in 2002 and 2003, he played in 15 All-Star Games, and was named MVP of the 2000 contest.

Still, with his incredible on-court accomplishments, Duncan is often overlooked when talking about the game's greatest players. One reason for this is that San Antonio is a small, relatively quiet city, with less media. Spurs players aren't household names for more casual fans. But ask any of Duncan's former teammates or coaches who they would want to have the ball with the game on the line and they would all pick number 21. Longtime teammate Tony Parker credited Duncan with making everyone he played with better players, saying, "that's the true definition of a superstar."

One moment proved his superstar status above all others, on New Year's Eve, 2014. The Spurs were hosting the New Orleans Pelicans, and with the game tied at 82, Pelicans' star Anthony Davis grabbed a rebound and dunked the ball, giving the Pelicans the lead. With just seven-tenths of a second left on the clock, the game was seemingly over.

San Antonio took a time-out, allowing for the inbounds pass at the other end of the court. Scoring with less than one second is impossible . . . unless you have Tim

Duncan. Duncan broke for the basket and teammate Boris Diaw lobbed a perfect high pass. The big man leaped for the basket and tipped the ball to the hoop. It rolled around the rim and fell in just as the clock expired! The game was going into overtime (OT). There, Duncan added three more points and the Spurs ended 2014 with a thrilling overtime win, 95–93.

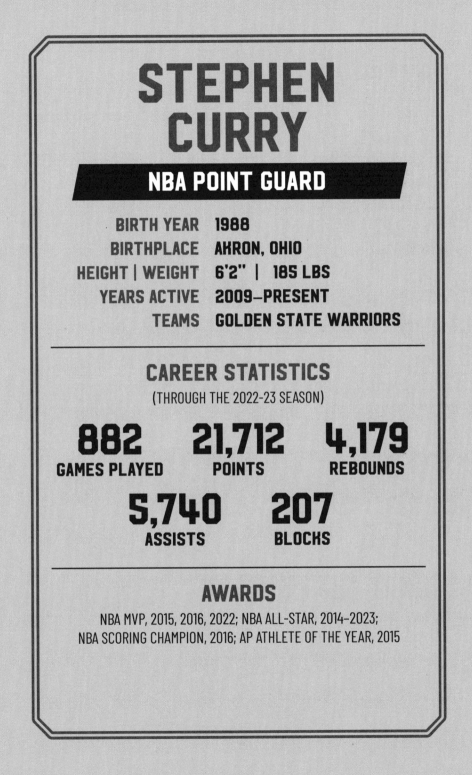

STEPHEN CURRY

NBA POINT GUARD

BIRTH YEAR	1988
BIRTHPLACE	AKRON, OHIO
HEIGHT	WEIGHT	6'2"	185 LBS
YEARS ACTIVE	2009–PRESENT
TEAMS	GOLDEN STATE WARRIORS

CAREER STATISTICS
(THROUGH THE 2022-23 SEASON)

882
GAMES PLAYED

21,712
POINTS

4,179
REBOUNDS

5,740
ASSISTS

207
BLOCKS

AWARDS

NBA MVP, 2015, 2016, 2022; NBA ALL-STAR, 2014–2023;
NBA SCORING CHAMPION, 2016; AP ATHLETE OF THE YEAR, 2015

A UNANIMOUS MVP

Stephen Curry had been unstoppable on the court during the 2015–16 season. His 30.1 points per game were best in the league. He also led the league in steals, field goals, three-pointers, and in his free-throw percentage. His 402 three-point shots set the NBA record. No player had ever made 400 in a season. Curry dominated from start to finish, leading the Warriors to a 73–9 record and the top seed in the playoffs, and he was named the league MVP. But what made winning this MVP Award so historic?

Curry won the award with an overwhelming, never-before-seen dominance. The NBA MVP was chosen by a panel of 130 sportswriters in the United States and Canada. Fans were also given the chance to vote for their MVP. In more than 60 seasons, no player had ever been a unanimous selection—until Curry. The best three-point shooter to play in the NBA, he earned the nod from all 130 sportswriters and the fans. As of 2023, he remains the only unanimous MVP in the history of the award.

CURRY THE MAGICIAN

Steph Curry was having a career night on the road against the Oklahoma City Thunder in 2016. After trailing by 11 points at the half, Curry led the charge as the

FAST FACTS

- No. 7 overall pick in the 2009 NBA Draft

- In 2015–2016 became only the second player in NBA history to average 30 PPG with a shooting percentage of .650

- Played on four NBA Championship teams with the Golden State Warriors (2015, 2017, 2018, 2022)

Warriors fought back. The Thunder were playing strong in front of the home crowd and with less than 3 minutes left in the game they held a seven-point lead. As Curry brought the ball up the court, he was looking for a teammate to pass to. Finding none, he pulled up from long distance and launched a three-pointer and drained it, cutting the Thunder's lead to only four points. A minute later, with his team trailing by five, Curry duplicated the long-range three-pointer, bringing the Warriors within two points. Golden State completed the comeback and tied the game at 103–103 to force overtime.

In overtime, Curry took over. He scored his team's first seven points in the extra frame. Despite his dominance and the fact that Thunder superstar (and future teammate) Kevin Durant had fouled out early in OT, the game was tied 118–118 with less than 30 seconds to go. After the

Thunder failed to score on the next possession, Golden State's Andre Iguodala grabbed the rebound. The stage was set for Curry magic . . . and he didn't disappoint.

Curry took the pass from Iguodala and pushed it up the court. As the clock wound down, Warriors coach Steve Kerr elected not to use his final time-out. He was putting the game in his superstar's hands. Curry crossed half-court, dribbled once, and launched a long three-pointer. With six-tenths of a second left, the ball banked in, and the Warriors won the game.

In a game where Curry set the new NBA record for most three-pointers made in a season, he had saved the most important one for the final second of the game!

A GOLDEN TOUCH

Wardell Stephen Curry II (Curry's legal name) is the second greatest basketball player born in Akron, Ohio, after The King, LeBron James. He grew up around the game, and with a father who played pro ball and a mom who was a collegiate volleyball player, Curry and his younger brother, Seth, were destined to be athletes. The boys grew up on NBA courts, shooting around with their father and his teammates. "I remember every game I went to," Curry said in a 2015 interview. "My dad was always a great role model for me."

Curry may have earned his golden touch at the three-point line from watching his dad. Dell Curry knocked down more than 1,200 three-point shots during his career. Steph, known for his quick release when he gets the ball in his hands, also got that from the man he calls "Pop."

In a 2009 conversation with Steph, Dell recounts, "I wasn't quick, and I couldn't jump, so I had to get it off the best way I could, the fastest way I could," explaining where his quick-release style came from. Growing up, Curry studied his dad and learned the game, whether it was at his father's team practices or at home in the family's driveway.

His father's NBA career meant the Currys moved around a bit. Steph was born in Ohio, raised in North Carolina, spent time in Toronto, and returned to Charlotte once Dell retired. Through it all, basketball was the common denominator. Still, even with his father as his mentor, early on it looked like Steph might not have the body for the game.

In his high school freshman season at Charlotte Christian School, Curry stood only five feet seven and weighed just 130 pounds. (He was so small that he couldn't wear number 30, his dad's NBA number. The team's number 30 jersey only came in extra-large and was way too big for Curry, so he had to settle on number 20.) Because of his size, he didn't even try out for the varsity squad, opting to play junior varsity instead. In 2015, he called that decision a mistake. "One of my only regrets is not trying out [for varsity] that year," he said. "That taught me to go for it. To not let what people might tell you—no matter how short or skinny you might be—deter you from getting where you want to go."

But as Curry grew, so too did his basketball skills. After a lone season playing junior varsity, Curry led the varsity squad for the next three seasons, winning three state championships and turning his success into a scholarship offer to play locally at Davidson College in North Carolina.

Curry dominated at Davidson, starting all three years, and leaving the school as its all-time leading scorer. By 2009, the kid who was too small to make his high school varsity team was ready to go pro!

SLOW, STEADY START

Following his decision to declare for the 2009 NBA Draft, some still said that Curry was too small to succeed in the NBA. His ball handling and shooting were unquestioned, but would his body be able to hold up to the grind and the physical nature of the NBA game? The Golden State Warriors thought so. They used the seventh pick in the first round of the 2009 Draft to make Curry a Warrior.

While some players may begin their careers unhappy with the team that drafted them, Curry was excited to be a Warrior from the start. At his opening press conference, he talked about the thrill it was to take his game to the professional level. "I see Golden State as a great fit for the way I play, and the direction this team is going." Seated alongside Warriors general manager Larry Riley at that opening press conference, Curry had no way of knowing that he was the critical piece in what was to become the next great NBA dynasty!

After Curry's introduction to the league, the Warriors continued to struggle, missing the playoffs in each of his first three seasons. Curry's transition to the NBA wasn't as immediately dominant as, say, LeBron's. It took the future Hall of Famer four seasons before he averaged more than 20 points in a season. In the 2011–12 campaign, for instance, he missed more than 50 games due to a potentially career-ending ankle injury. Luckily, the medical staff was able to help Curry. Since then, his ankle has held up and he has gone on to become arguably the best shooter in the NBA.

With his health at peak form, Curry took his game to the next level in the 2012–13 season. Curry averaged almost 23 points per game, and the Warriors broke through with their first playoff appearance in six years. Though they were knocked out by the Denver Nuggets in the first round of the playoffs, Golden State had arrived—and they've never left.

SAVING A FRANCHISE

Steph Curry will be remembered as a player who helped reignite the passion for basketball for an entire city. Before the Warriors drafted Curry in the first round of the 2009 NBA Draft, the franchise had missed the playoffs 14 out of its previous 15 seasons. The team was bad, the fan base was disinterested, and the future looked grim. In his 14 years with Golden State, Curry has led the Warriors to the playoffs nine times. The team appeared in six NBA Finals, collecting four NBA titles. He's responsible for saving the Warriors franchise.

Beyond the titles, Curry brings a level of excitement to every game. Curry is so electric when he's shooting three-pointers that even non-fans tune in to watch him in action. His ability to make a basket from anywhere on the court, anytime in the game, makes every second of Warriors' basketball must-watch television.

In 2019, Curry was asked about his legacy. "Whenever [people] ask me about legacy . . . I don't know. I don't want to ruin the moment," he said on the *Today* show. In the humble fashion he's known for, the Warriors leader dismissed any talk of being one of the all-time greats. "I feel like the way I got here was by keeping my head down and grinding," he said. "I'm not going to switch that up."

When he finally decides to leave the game behind, Steph Curry will be a shoo-in for the Hall of Fame. He will be the greatest player in Golden State's history. And he will be remembered for playing the game hard and always seeming to have fun doing it.

SUE BIRD

WNBA POINT GUARD

BIRTH YEAR **1980**
BIRTHPLACE **SYOSSET, NEW YORK**
HEIGHT | WEIGHT **5'9" | 150 LBS**
YEARS ACTIVE **2002–2022**
TEAMS **SEATTLE STORM**

CAREER STATISTICS
(THROUGH THE 2022 SEASON)

416
GAMES PLAYED

4,730
POINTS

990
REBOUNDS

2,300
ASSISTS

52
BLOCKS

AWARDS

WNBA ALL-STAR, 2002, 2003, 2005–2007, 2009, 2011, 2014, 2015, 2017, 2018, 2021, 2022; WNBA TOP 15 PLAYERS OF ALL-TIME; WNBA ALL-DECADE TEAM; WNBA CHAMPION, 2004, 2010, 2018, 2020; RUSSIAN NATIONAL LEAGUE CHAMPION, 2007, 2008, 2012–14; NCAA CHAMPION, 2000, 2002; OLYMPIC GOLD MEDALIST 2004, 2008, 2012, 2016, 2020

BIRD AT THE BUZZER

It was the final game in the 2001 Big East Championship; the UConn Huskies faced off against the Notre Dame Fighting Irish in a showcase game that pitted two powerhouse women's basketball schools against each other. After a back-and-forth battle, with just 38 seconds left in the game, UConn held a 76–75 lead and had possession. Sue Bird, then a junior at UConn, worked the ball around the perimeter. Bird's job was to chew up time on the clock, but she made a costly mistake that gave Notre Dame possession with 16 seconds to go. Notre Dame center Ruth Riley drove to the basket with a chance to win the game but drew a hard foul. Riley missed the first free throw, then sank the second to tie the game at 76 with 5.1 seconds to go. The Huskies had five seconds to claim their victory.

Bird took the inbounds pass. It was clear she had no plans to bring the game into overtime—she was looking to make up for her earlier mistake. Bird sprinted up the court and pulled up for the game-winning jump shot. The ball rattled off the front of the rim and fell in! Her teammates mobbed Bird on the court to celebrate their 2001 Big East title.

Two decades later, the game and Bird's shot are remembered as one of the biggest games and biggest moments in women's college basketball history. The game was even immortalized in a book called *Bird at the Buzzer*. For Bird, with all of her on-court accomplishments—from WNBA

FAST FACTS

- No. 1 pick in the 2002 WNBA Draft
- Wore number 10 because she and her sister were born in October
- All-time WNBA leader in games played

Championship titles to Olympic gold medals—"the shot" is still the play she will forever be remembered for and is most often asked about.

EXCELLENCE UNDER PRESSURE

At the end of the 2010 season, more than 15,000 screaming fans were on their feet as the Seattle Storm found themselves in the biggest moment of the WNBA season. It was Game 1 of the finals and Seattle was hosting the Atlanta Dream. The game was knotted at 77–77, with the clock winding down. The Storm had one last chance to end the game in regulation—without going into overtime—and they drew up a play that would put the ball in the hands of Sue Bird to win it.

During the regular season, Bird was only third on the team in scoring. Her 11.1 points per game trailed teammates Lauren Jackson (20.5) and Swin Cash (13.8). Jackson had the hot hand in Game 1, dropping 26 points to lead all scorers. While Bird played a strong game, her stat line read just 12 points scored. But when the game was on the line, Storm coach Brian Agler wanted Bird taking the final shot.

Bird brought the ball to the top of the court as the clock ran under five seconds. She dribbled, pulled up, and jumped. Bird sank the pressure-packed bucket with just 2.6 seconds left to give the Storm the Game 1 win!

After the win, Bird was asked why she seemed to perform so well in those high-pressure situations. "You get confidence, the more you do things, and the more you are successful," she said in the postgame press conference. "At this point in my career, it's something I enjoy. Those situations are fun."

The game-winning shot gave Seattle all of the momentum in the best of five series. Two nights later they won 87–84, finishing an undefeated season at home and posting a perfect 21–0 record. After shutting down the Dream in Atlanta to complete the series sweep, Bird collected her second WNBA Championship title. She was asked after the game what it meant to her. "It's been a long time since 2004 [the Storm's last title] and to get back, to win, to go undefeated in the playoffs and have the best record, I couldn't be happier."

RIGHT CHOICES

Sue Bird was born in Syosset, New York, in 1980 and is the youngest of two. Bird credits her older sister, Jen, with getting her interested in playing basketball when she was seven years old. "I looked up to Jen," Bird said in an interview for UConn Hoop Legends' website. "I wanted to do whatever Jen did."

After two years of playing varsity basketball at Syosset High School, Bird's parents made the decision to move their daughter to a private school to focus on her basketball game. Christ the King Regional High School had a reputation for sending players to the pros. NBA stars Lamar Odom and Jayson Williams and WNBA stars Tina Charles and Chamique Holdsclaw all graduated from the school.

The decision to transfer proved to be the right one for Bird. She excelled at Christ the King, with the team going undefeated at 27–0 in her first season and winning the New York State Championship. During her senior season in 1997–98, the Royals once again went undefeated. Bird averaged more than 16 points, seven rebounds, and eight steals per game. The team captured its second state championship and Bird was named New York State Player of the Year.

Bird's play drew the interest of scouts from across the country. She had offers to play at some of the best schools in the nation, including the University of Connecticut and Stanford University. In the end, Bird says she liked the idea of staying close to home, so she chose to become a UConn Husky.

Like the decision to transfer to Christ the King, Bird's choice of UConn again proved to be the right one. She joined one of the most prestigious programs in women's college basketball. Over the next four years, she would be an integral part of the Huskies' success—UConn went an incredible 136–9. She won two National Championships, including capping off an undefeated senior season by winning her second crown.

"When we won the national championship, it was just a lot of emotion, a lot of feeling," Bird said in an interview for WNBA.com. "It was my four-year career in college coming down to this one moment where we go unde-feated, win a national championship, and we're on top. That was just a great feeling." It was also the perfect way to end her college career and prepare for life in the pros.

THE STORY WITH STATS

In 2000 and 2001, the Seattle Storm had a combined record of 16–48. They won just 10 games in 2001, earning the top pick in the 2002 WNBA Draft. The team used that pick to select Sue Bird. For Bird, it was the culmination of years of hard work. Two high schools and a four-year college career had netted Bird four titles, and now it had earned her the distinction of being the number one pick in the WNBA draft.

Six weeks later, Bird took the court for her first professional game. The Storm were hosting the New York Liberty, and Bird was starting at guard. The rookie wasted no time establishing herself as worthy of the top pick. She led all scorers in the game with 18 points and added seven rebounds and a pair of assists. The Storm lost Bird's first game, 78–61, but with her strong play they won 17 games that year—more than the previous two seasons combined.

Bird built on her impressive rookie season, in which she earned the first of 11 All-Star Game appearances, by coming back with a strong sophomore campaign in 2003. Overall, Bird's pro career is defined by winning, even while her numbers have never been eye-popping. In 18 seasons in Seattle, Bird has only led the team in scoring twice. Her 12.1 points per game average might not scare anyone, but those who have played with her and against her know that Bird can't be defined by statistics. She was a key part of the Storm's four WNBA Championships (2004, 2010, 2018, and 2020). She has also built a solid career playing overseas during the WNBA off-season.

Though she missed the entire 2019 season after suffering a knee injury, Bird has been incredibly reliable throughout her career. She was the all-time leader in games played in WNBA history and assists. Bird was also in the top 10 in career points scored.

A LEGACY TO MODEL

On June 16, 2022, Bird announced that she would be retiring at the end of the 2022 season. Like many of the trailblazing stars of the WNBA, her legacy will be two-part.

On the court, Bird has made her case for being one of the best of all time. The 13-time All-Star has won at every level. She collected a pair of state championships in high school, then followed up with two NCAA Championships as a member of the UConn Huskies. Bird next collected four titles as the leader of the Seattle Storm. If that isn't enough, she's won five Olympic gold medals earned as a member of Team USA.

Off the court, Bird has an equally strong presence. She has joined the fight for pay equality for WNBA players. She has spent a decade playing overseas in the off-season, something she says is necessary due to the relatively low salaries she and her teammates earn. "Look, we're not over here saying we should be paid the same as the men," Bird said in a 2019 interview with *Ms.* magazine. "We understand that this is a business and that their revenue is insane compared to ours, but there is a bias that exists." She continues to work tirelessly to educate the public about that bias.

Bird has also become a public figure in the fight for gay rights. In 2019, she and her now-wife, soccer star Megan Rapinoe, shared the cover of *ESPN the Magazine*'s annual Body Issue. It was the first time a same-sex couple had graced the cover of the popular magazine. Bird said she hopes the couple has paved the way for others to follow. "I think having a gay couple on [the cover], hopefully it just becomes the norm," she said in a 2019 interview with ESPN. "You want it to just be, 'Oh, another couple is on there.' You know, I think for us to be on it is the first step in that direction." For Bird, it is another feather in her cap as she builds a legacy that reaches beyond the basketball court.

Honorable Mentions POINT GUARD

RUSSELL WESTBROOK

Westbrook has benefitted from playing alongside Kevin Durant and James Harden for much of his career. But although he may have taken a back seat to the higher-profile players on his teams, Westbrook has consistently delivered superstar-level stats over the last decade. The nine-time All-Star and two-time scoring champion was a steady force for the Oklahoma City Thunder from 2008 to 2019 before a surprise trade to the Houston Rockets. He has since played for the Washington Wizards, the Los Angeles Lakers, and the Los Angeles Clippers.

His biggest season was 2016–17, when Westbrook became only the second player in NBA history to average a triple-double for the season. He also collected the League MVP Award that year. Despite his great game, Westbrook has a lack of championship titles to his name.

Maybe in his defense, his former teammate Durant didn't win a title until he left Oklahoma City. Many believe that it is only a matter of time before Westbrook holds the NBA Championship trophy.

KYRIE IRVING

Despite the turmoil that seems to follow him around, Irving has remained a productive—sometimes even dominant—point guard over his career. His résumé includes eight All-Star Game appearances (he was named MVP of the 2014 game), a Rookie of the Year Award in 2012, and the ring he collected with LeBron in Cleveland in 2016. His career-long 23 points per game is solid, though he has yet to play a full 82-game slate since entering the NBA.

Paired with LeBron in Cleveland, Irving later forced his way out of town in a trade to the Boston Celtics. Soon he wore out his welcome in Boston and headed to Brooklyn, joining Kevin Durant on the Nets. Irving lit up his debut with the Nets, setting an NBA record for the most points scored in a debut (50). He was traded to the Dallas Mavericks in 2023.

No one questions Kyrie Irving's talent on the basketball court. Yet it's some of the baggage the Mavericks' newest superstar carries with him that relegates him to an honorable mention. He has a reputation for controversial opinions that he has no problem airing frequently during public interviews, even if he knows people will disagree. If he can ease his off-court drama and continue to post numbers like he does, he will soon silence his critics.

COURTNEY VANDERSLOOT

Basketball is a game that can breed selfishness. Players are judged by points scored, game-winning shots, and how many individual awards they win. That's what makes the career of New York Liberty point guard Courtney Vandersloot all the more impressive.

Vandersloot led the WNBA in assists in four of her twelve seasons with the Chicago Sky. She is the ultimate team player, setting the table for her teammates to score. In 2018, Vandersloot set the WNBA single season record for assists when she delivered 258. She quickly broke her own record in 2019, dropping 300 assists in the regular season and another 23 in two postseason contests. On a team filled with scoring machines, Courtney Vandersloot was the selfless teammate that made the Chicago Sky's offense run.

Legendary Great POINT GUARD

MAGIC JOHNSON

The Lakers–Celtics rivalry of the 1980s is arguably the most renowned in the history of professional sports. Magic Johnson, Kareem Abdul-Jabbar, and James Worthy squaring off against Larry Bird, Robert Parrish, and Kevin McHale made for some incredibly exciting games. The two teams won a combined eight titles in the '80s and, thanks in large part to the dominant play of Earvin "Magic" Johnson, the Lakers collected five of those rings.

Magic's stardom began long before the Lakers made him the first overall pick in the 1979 NBA Draft. He capped off his college career at Michigan State by leading the Spartans to the NCAA Championship, where he poured in 24 points and won the tournament's MVP award. His arrival in Los Angeles began the dynasty run of the Lakers.

On the court, Johnson was arguably the most commanding point guard of his era. As a rookie, he led the Lakers to an NBA Championship. His performance in Game 6 against the Eastern Conference Champion Philadelphia 76ers is legendary. Against the 76ers, Magic managed 42 points, 15 rebounds, and 7 assists, playing a game-high of 47 minutes. The Lakers knocked off the 76ers on their own court, 123–107, to win Magic's first title and his first Finals MVP Award.

At 20 years old, Johnson had already won a High School State Championship, an NCAA Championship, and an NBA Championship. And he was just getting warmed up. He would lead the Lakers to eight more appearances in the NBA Finals over his career, winning four more titles.

If you were only given one season to capture the greatness of Johnson's career, 1986–87 would be the year to choose. A case could be made that it was the best individual season in NBA history. Let's start with the pure stats: Johnson had career highs in games played (80) and points per game (23.9) and he led the league in assists (12.2). He was named to the All-Star Team for the sixth season in a row, he earned All-NBA First Team honors, and he was named league MVP.

But Magic's greatness went deeper than individual statistics. What made him so special was his ability to make his teammates better. He led the 1986–87 Lakers to a regular season record of 65–17, capturing the Pacific Division title. He then dominated in the playoffs as the Lakers went 11–1, defeating the Nuggets, Warriors, and Supersonics on the way to the NBA Finals and a matchup with the Celtics. For Johnson, it was showtime.

In a critical Game 1 win at home, Magic poured in 29 points. He went on to average 21 points and 12 rebounds per game, but it was the closing seconds of Game 4 that fans remember best. The Lakers trailed 106–105 with two seconds left. The Lakers inbounded to Johnson, and he looked to dish the ball off. The Celtics were playing tight and, with no other options, Johnson glided toward the paint and laid up a finger-roll hook shot. He knocked it down for the game-winner!

The crowd at the Boston Garden was stunned. The Lakers took the game 107–106 and won the series 4–2. Johnson collected his fourth ring and his third NBA Finals MVP Award. In eight years, he had transformed the Lakers into the most powerful dynasty in basketball!

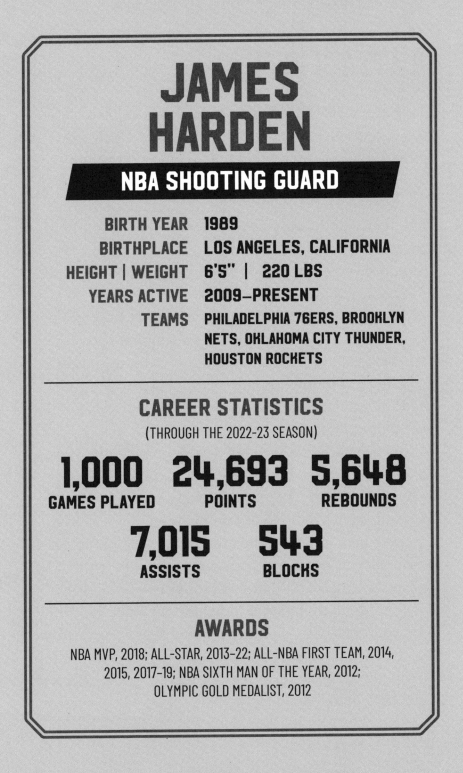

JAMES HARDEN

NBA SHOOTING GUARD

BIRTH YEAR **1989**
BIRTHPLACE **LOS ANGELES, CALIFORNIA**
HEIGHT | WEIGHT **6'5" | 220 LBS**
YEARS ACTIVE **2009–PRESENT**
TEAMS **PHILADELPHIA 76ERS, BROOKLYN NETS, OKLAHOMA CITY THUNDER, HOUSTON ROCKETS**

CAREER STATISTICS
(THROUGH THE 2022-23 SEASON)

1,000
GAMES PLAYED

24,693
POINTS

5,648
REBOUNDS

7,015
ASSISTS

543
BLOCKS

AWARDS

NBA MVP, 2018; ALL-STAR, 2013–22; ALL-NBA FIRST TEAM, 2014, 2015, 2017–19; NBA SIXTH MAN OF THE YEAR, 2012; OLYMPIC GOLD MEDALIST, 2012

IN ATTACK MODE

The San Antonio Spurs came to Houston on March 22, 2019, to take on their cross-state rivals, the Houston Rockets. The Spurs' starting lineup posted 71 points in the game—solid numbers on any night. Unless, of course, you run into a red-hot James Harden, who matched his career-high by dropping 61 on the visitors to lead a 111–105 win.

Harden was hot from the opening tip-off and never took his foot off the gas. He dropped 27 points in the opening quarter alone. The Spurs had no answer for the big man. If they left him open on the perimeter, he killed them with three-pointers, dropping nine in the game, including five in the first half. When San Antonio contested Harden and he drew fouls, he was incredible at the line, adding 14 points.

This was Harden's second 61-point game of the season. He had first accomplished the feat back in January, against the New York Knicks. In that game, Harden knocked down a handful of three-pointers, shot 22 from the free-throw line, and when the game was tight in the fourth quarter, he poured in 12 points to seal the win. The Rockets were playing shorthanded, with several players out nursing injuries. A thin bench meant extended playing time for Harden, and with more pressure to carry the team, he responded. "We're limited guys, so whatever I have to do to try to win games, I'll do it, and Coach knows that," he said following the win.

FAST FACTS

- No. 3 overall pick in the 2009 NBA Draft

- NBA's all-time leader in 50-point triple-doubles

- Averaged at least 34 points, 7 assists, and 6 rebounds in both 2019 and 2020 (no other player has done so in NBA history)

HARDEN'S RAINBOW BALL

James Harden (aka "the Beard") was having another monster offensive night for the Rockets in 2019. In the game, the Beard had scored 33 points on the road against the defending NBA Champion Golden State Warriors. Harden had buried seven three-pointers and led all scorers for the game. Still, the Warriors—led by Steph Curry who scored 35 points—tied the game at 119–119 and forced it into overtime. Faced with the Warriors front three of Curry, Kevin Durant, and Klay Thompson, would the Rockets be able to steal a road win in OT?

A back-and-forth battle in overtime saw each team put up 13 points, and with 33 seconds left in the first overtime period the game was tied up at 132–132. The Warriors were driving, but Kevin Durant lost the ball. As it went out of bounds, Durant dove, swatting the ball back into play and saving the possession. The ball went out to Curry, who took two dribbles and buried a jumper to give the Warriors the lead, 134–132. After a loose ball out of bounds, the Rockets prepared to inbound the ball with 5.5 seconds on the clock. Gerald Green was inbounding for Houston, and he was looking at Harden. Harden took the pass and tried to work free for a shot.

As the clock wound down, Harden went high in the air, extending over the double coverage from members of the other team, and launched a "rainbow ball"—a shot that has a higher-than-normal arc—over both Warriors. The shot rattled in with one second on the clock and the Rockets won big thanks to the heroics of Harden!

Harden finished with a game-high 44 points, including 11 in the overtime frame. After the game, Harden was asked what it takes to deliver when the moment calls for it. "[It takes] the work," Harden said. "Yesterday I was in that same spot [in practice] shooting that same shot, so I had confidence it was going to go in."

A WAY OUT

Growing up in Compton, California, Harden began his athletic career in baseball, not basketball. After his stint on the diamond, Harden came to the court at age 10. Soon, he was playing year-round, whether in a local league or at home on a hoop nailed to the garage.

In a 2017 interview, Harden's mom, Monja Willis, talked about the importance of sports in the lives of the future NBA star and his older brother when they were kids. "By keeping them active in sports, that kept them out of gangs," she explained. "Anybody can come in and try to take advantage of them. That's why I focused on sports for them. They ended up loving it."

As a child, Harden battled asthma, a big challenge for a basketball player—the game demands a lot of cardio endurance. Sports helped the young Harden get in better shape and gradually he got his asthma under control.

By the time he reached high school, Harden was fixated on basketball. He would leave his house early most mornings, arriving at his school by 7:00 a.m. so he could work out in the gym before class. It is a work ethic that Harden maintains today as an established NBA superstar.

Those around him, including his mom, began to sense Harden might have what it takes to be something special on the basketball court. "I saw potential then," his mom told TheAthletic.com in a 2017 interview. "I didn't really like basketball or like sports, period. But I knew my kids had to do something to keep their mind busy." For Harden, sports—basketball in particular—were his road out of the tough streets of Compton.

After winning back-to-back state titles while at Artesia High School in Lakewood, California, and adding a Las Vegas Adidas Super 64 Championship in 2006, Harden was recruited to play basketball for Arizona State University. His career as a Sun Devil was short. After two seasons, during which he earned All-American honors and was named Pac-10 Player of the Year in 2009, Harden was ready to take the next step in his basketball journey. The kid from Compton was ready for the NBA.

FROM BENCH PLAYER TO STAR

"With the third pick in the 2009 NBA Draft, the Oklahoma City Thunder select James Harden of Arizona State University." With those words on June 25, 2009, NBA Commissioner David Stern made it official—James Harden was a professional basketball player!

But even on draft night the young James Harden wasn't lacking confidence in his game. "I don't think I need to prove anything," he said when asked about those who doubted the Thunder's decision to draft him so high. "I just need to go in there, work hard, and try my best to earn a spot on that team."

Unlike many high draft picks who are thrust into the starting lineup immediately, Harden began his career as a bench player. He didn't play a single game in his rookie season of 2009–10. In fact, the future league scoring champion only started in seven games in three seasons with Oklahoma. Still, his game developed and improved. His strong play off the bench earned him the NBA Sixth Man Award. It also earned him an opportunity to move into a starting role—just not with the Thunder. On October 27, 2012, the Thunder announced they had traded Harden to the Houston Rockets. In Houston, Harden would sign an $80-million contract and become a starter for the first time in his NBA career.

The three-year bench player started 78 games in his first season in Houston, averaging an impressive 25.8 points per game. He also greatly improved on the dismal playoff performances that had become a sore spot for him in Oklahoma City. Harden seemed to disappear when the postseason arrived for the Thunder. In Houston, at least by the numbers, he delivered: He averaged more than 26 points per game in his first postseason as a Rocket.

Seven years into his tenure in Houston, Harden had developed into a premier shooter and one of the biggest offensive threats in the league. He was named to the All-Star Game in all seven of his seasons in Houston and won the scoring title in back-to-back seasons.

But it was 2018 when it all came together. Harden broke the 30-point-per-game barrier for the first time in his career, averaging 30.2 for the season. He added nearly nine assists per game and led the Rockets to the Western Conference Finals. Though they came up short, losing the series 4–3 to the eventual NBA Champion Golden State Warriors, Harden ended the season with his first NBA MVP Award.

A COMPLEX LEGACY

Earlier in his career with Oklahoma City, and early in his time in Houston, Harden developed a reputation as a player who couldn't deliver in the playoffs. Sure, his final stats in a game might look good, but in the fourth quarter when the team looked to Harden to lock it down, he missed with alarming frequency.

In 2015, Harden's Rockets were taking on the Golden State Warriors in the Western Conference Finals. With the Warriors leading the Series 3–1, Game 5 was do-or-die for the Rockets. When they needed him most, Harden delivered a record-breaking night—the kind of record you don't want to break. Harden turned the ball over 13 times, an NBA record, as the Warriors cruised to a 104–90 win to advance to the NBA Finals.

How James Harden will be remembered is complex. The Beard is still busy overpowering the NBA, most recently with his trades to the Brooklyn Nets in 2021, the Philadelphia 76ers in 2022, and the Los Angeles Clippers in 2023. He is one of the most feared offensive weapons of his era, the man who came second in the league in scoring (after Steph Curry) for three seasons in a row, and one of the most dominant shooters in the league. Harden's critics say his numbers are padded by what is seen as a selfish style of play. Still, Harden's talent prevails.

DIANA TAURASI

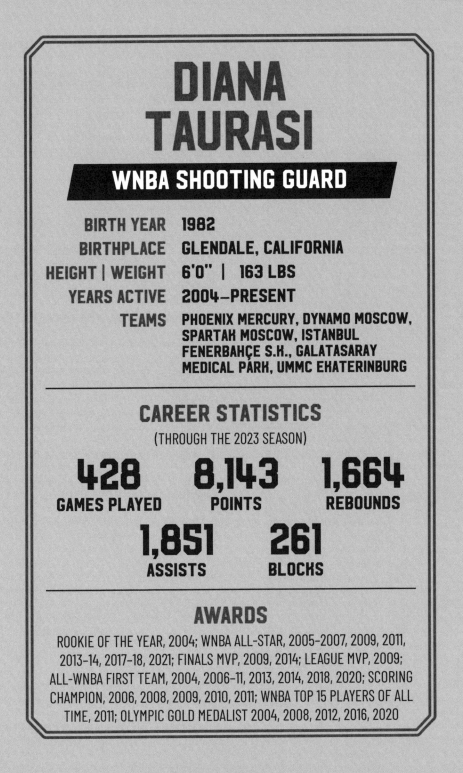

WNBA SHOOTING GUARD

BIRTH YEAR	1982
BIRTHPLACE	GLENDALE, CALIFORNIA
HEIGHT | WEIGHT	6'0" | 163 LBS
YEARS ACTIVE	2004–PRESENT
TEAMS	PHOENIX MERCURY, DYNAMO MOSCOW, SPARTAK MOSCOW, ISTANBUL FENERBAHÇE S.K., GALATASARAY MEDICAL PARK, UMMC EKATERINBURG

CAREER STATISTICS

(THROUGH THE 2023 SEASON)

428
GAMES PLAYED

8,143
POINTS

1,664
REBOUNDS

1,851
ASSISTS

261
BLOCKS

AWARDS

ROOKIE OF THE YEAR, 2004; WNBA ALL-STAR, 2005–2007, 2009, 2011, 2013–14, 2017–18, 2021; FINALS MVP, 2009, 2014; LEAGUE MVP, 2009; ALL-WNBA FIRST TEAM, 2004, 2006–11, 2013, 2014, 2018, 2020; SCORING CHAMPION, 2006, 2008, 2009, 2010, 2011; WNBA TOP 15 PLAYERS OF ALL TIME, 2011; OLYMPIC GOLD MEDALIST 2004, 2008, 2012, 2016, 2020

BEST LONG RANGE SHOOTER

The Phoenix Mercury were in an early 8–0 hole on the road against the Chicago Sky. The Mercury needed a spark, and Diana Taurasi gave it to them. They knew a record was going to be made that night.

As the Mercury moved the ball around looking for a clean shot against the aggressive Sky defense, Taurasi quietly slid out to three-point range. That's where teammate Danielle Robinson found her and delivered a crisp pass. Taurasi didn't hesitate; she never even put the ball on the floor. She turned and released the quick shot before the Sky defender even had a chance to get into position. She buried the three-pointer, and the record was broken—Diana Taurasi was now the all-time leading three-point shooter in WNBA history!

Though it was the 907th three-point shot of her WNBA career, when the shot dropped, it was just another bucket for the WNBA champion. She took a quick high-five from a teammate before jogging back on defense. She didn't come to Chicago to set personal records; she came to win the game.

Her record-setting three-pointer put Taurasi in a groove. She delivered her most dominating offensive performance in seven seasons, dropping 37 points on the Sky. She led her team back from the early deficit and returned to Phoenix with a 99–91 win.

With the victory secured, Taurasi allowed herself to reflect on her accomplishment. "Passing Katie Smith

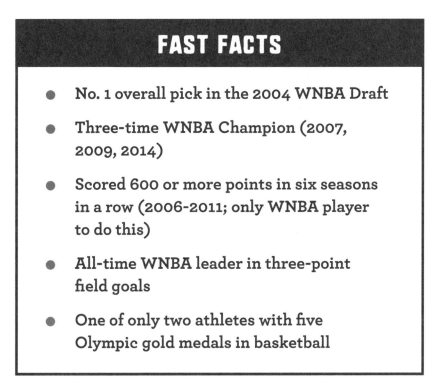

FAST FACTS

- No. 1 overall pick in the 2004 WNBA Draft

- Three-time WNBA Champion (2007, 2009, 2014)

- Scored 600 or more points in six seasons in a row (2006-2011; only WNBA player to do this)

- All-time WNBA leader in three-point field goals

- One of only two athletes with five Olympic gold medals in basketball

[for career three-pointers made] is something I never thought would happen," Taurasi said in an interview following the big win. "She was one of my heroes growing up. I got a chance to share the court with her at the Olympics, and she taught me how to be a professional."

The following season, Taurasi became the first player in WNBA history to reach 1,000 career three-pointers. She has continued to add to that total, proving to be the most efficient, effective long-range shooter the WNBA has ever seen.

WNBA'S LEADING SCORER

The WNBA is a league driven by scoring. Fans love offense, and Taurasi has provided a ton of it during her career; so it seems fitting to look to the offensive side of the ball to highlight her biggest moment in basketball.

It was June 2018. Taurasi's Mercury were on the road to take on the Los Angeles Sparks. It was barely a week since Taurasi broke the WNBA three-point record. Tonight, she was on track for the ultimate individual mark: the chance to become the all-time leading scorer in league history. Taurasi's family and friends, along with a strong showing of Mercury fans, had traveled to L.A. for the historic night. There was a playoff vibe in the air. Lakers great Kobe Bryant sat courtside.

Just before halftime, with her team trailing by 19 points, Taurasi made history. For the league's leading three-point shooter, it was ironic that she set the scoring record by driving the lane and rolling a layup off the glass and in. The game was stopped to celebrate Taurasi's accomplishment. Though she looked ready to get back to work, players from both teams offered on-court congratulations and she was presented with the ball. At the end of the game, Taurasi had amassed a career-total 7,494 points, passing Tina Thompson's mark of 7,488.

The Sparks spoiled Taurasi's big night, handing the Mercury a 90–59 loss. After the game, Taurasi deflected much of the praise away from herself. "It's pretty special when you pass Tina in anything, she's been such an amazing player for the WNBA and just for basketball in general, she's such an icon," Taurasi said. "And when you start thinking about . . . more of the people that you've shared the court with, the coaches, the teams, you know I've been pretty lucky to be around a lot of great players."

A KID FROM CHINO

Had things gone just a tiny bit differently, Diana Taurasi may never have scored a single WNBA point. Taurasi jokes that she could have ended up playing soccer for the United States Women's National Team. If it sounds impossible to imagine the WNBA's all-time leading scorer racing up and down a soccer pitch, consider her family history.

Taurasi's parents, Mario and Liliana, hail from the soccer-obsessed country of Argentina. She and her older sister, Jessika, were raised in Chino, California, and they played both basketball and soccer. "The truth is, I liked soccer more," Taurasi wrote in an article for the Players' Tribune. "But my dad, knowing and encouraging, said, 'Diana. Go play basketball.'"

Taurasi didn't play organized basketball until she was in sixth grade, and it didn't take long for people to realize she was special. "In eighth grade, I got my first letter of recruitment . . . from Walla Walla Washington Community College. I was like, 'That's it! This is amazing. That's where I'm going,'" she wrote. "But more came— almost every single day. I'd go to the mailbox, and there would be letters from 10, 12 schools. Places I didn't even know. *Where's Drexel? Where's Hofstra?* I had no clue. I was just a kid from Chino."

After a stellar high school career, during which she was named the Naismith Player of the Year in 2000, Taurasi had to choose. One thing was certain: She was going to attend a Division I college on a full basketball scholarship. The only question was ... where?

Her dad wanted her to play at UConn; her mom preferred she stay closer to home. Taurasi followed her dad's advice and traded California for Connecticut to become a Husky. It turned out to be the best decision of her career. She would lead UConn to the Final Four in all four of her seasons as a Husky, winning three National titles in a row. She was named Most Outstanding Player of the tournament in 2003 and 2004. Not bad for, as she liked to describe herself, "just a kid from Chino."

In 2004, UConn basketball was the talk of the sports world and Taurasi was the crown jewel of the program. That's why it came as no surprise when the Phoenix Mercury used the number one pick in the 2004 WNBA Draft to bring Taurasi to Arizona.

LEADER ON THE COURT

Professional sports usually offer a short career. Players who do stick around often do so by jumping from team to team, filling the needs of different organizations. The Mercury coaches and executives could never have imagined when they signed Taurasi that 19 years later she would still be with the organization and performing at an elite level. It was, in hindsight, the best draft pick in league history.

Fittingly, the first shot she took—and made—in her career was a three-pointer. She showed her versatility with several nifty assists, three blocks, and an awe-inspiring half-court shot that she drained at the buzzer before the half. The Mercury fell short in the game, but it was clear to the more than 10,000 fans that packed the arena that something special had come to Phoenix.

From her rookie season forward, Taurasi established herself as the undisputed leader of the Mercury. Her head coach, Sandy Brondello, speaks regularly about what it means to have Taurasi on the squad. "Diana Taurasi is just amazing," Brondello says. "She's a great leader and she'll lead through action, or she'll lead though constructive criticism or motivation. Whatever it takes, that's what she'll do. She'll drive people to get better."

Look at Game 3 of the 2014 WNBA Finals. Taurasi's Mercury led Elena Delle Donne's Chicago Sky 3–2 in the best of five series. But the Sky were at home for Game 3, hoping to keep the series alive. The two teams battled it out for 39 minutes, and with the game tied at 82–82, with less than 20 seconds left on the clock, both teams needed a clutch play. Taurasi delivered.

Bringing the ball up the court, any other player might have been tempted to stay on the perimeter, milk the clock, and look for a long-range shot for the game-winner. Instead, Taurasi drove to the basket for a tough pull-up jumper. In a hostile environment, with an aggressive defender on her and the game on the line, Taurasi delivered the game-winner! Adding icing to the cake, she drew a foul and converted the three-point play, giving the Mercury the 85–82 lead. With the Mercury star center Brittney Griner out with an injury, Taurasi put the team on her back and delivered her third title to Phoenix!

GLOBE-SPANNING CAREER

To play professional basketball for a single game means you are an elite athlete and one of the best players in the world. Taurasi has played at the highest level for *two decades*. Her game is a tribute to her physical gifts, her mental toughness, and her passion. When examining her legacy, her value is in her longevity.

Taurasi is a proven winner. She's won championships in four different professional leagues. In addition to leading the Mercury to the WNBA Championship title three times, she was part of seven title-winning teams in the Russian National League, she collected six trophies in the EuroLeague, and she won a title in the Turkish National League in 2011. Add in her three National Championships at UConn and Taurasi is one of the most decorated basketball players in history.

Like so many of her peers in women's basketball, Taurasi is also known for her advocacy work. She has long been outspoken for LGBTQIA+ rights, and more recently she has joined the fight for more equitable pay. In 2019, Taurasi earned the league maximum salary of

$117,500 playing for the Mercury. That year, she also earned $1.5 million playing in the Russian National League. Taurasi has been one of the most vocal players in the WNBA when it comes to criticizing the pay scale.

Taurasi was the first WNBA star to sit out a full WNBA season because of salary. In 2015, her Russian squad, UMMC Ekaterinburg, requested that she sit out the WNBA season to rest her body. Considering the Russian team paid her roughly 14 times more than the WNBA, it seemed like a reasonable request. Taurasi sat, and that will forever be etched in her legacy. She was called selfish by fans, who accused her of quitting on her teammates. But within the league, she received support from other players for her decision to protect herself and her career first.

Nevertheless, Taurasi is known for her unending drive. She has battled her way back from hip, back, and ankle injuries, always pushing herself harder in rehab to rejoin her teammates. The injuries are thought to be caused, in part, by the year-round schedule she keeps. In addition to her superstar career overseas, she also plays in extended seasons in the WNBA when Phoenix makes the playoffs. The wear and tear on her body adds up.

When she steps away from the game, Diana Taurasi will be remembered as one of the best—if not *the* best— to play in the WNBA. She will be remembered for her deadly three-point shooting ability, her passion for the game of basketball and her teammates, and her ability to win wherever she goes. She will be remembered by many as simply the G.O.A.T.

Honorable Mentions SHOOTING GUARD

DONOVAN MITCHELL

As the youngest player in this book, Mitchell earns a spot among the game's greats by virtue of the red-hot start to his NBA career. As a rookie, Mitchell started 71 games for the Utah Jazz in 2017–18, posting more than 20 points per game. Historically, rookies can wear down by the end of the long NBA season and then struggle in the playoffs. For Mitchell, it was just the opposite. In the 2017–18 playoffs, he lit it up, putting up 171 points in the first playoff series of his career. Only Kareem Abdul-Jabbar and Wilt Chamberlain posted better scoring numbers to begin their playoff careers.

Jazz coach Quin Snyder offered high praise for Mitchell's game during his first trip to the playoffs. "I [didn't] see Donovan as a rookie for the most part, for the whole season," Snyder said, "because of the way he's played and the poise he's had . . . the way he's elevated his teammates."

Mitchell's strong start wasn't a one-hit wonder. He came back in the 2019 playoffs, scoring 21 points per game. Through his first two seasons, Mitchell averaged 23.4 points per game in the postseason. Mitchell looks to be one of the exciting players to watch in the NBA for years to come.

JRUE HOLIDAY

While many of the players in this book are noted for their offensive abilities, Jrue Holiday is coveted for his defensive skills. The NBA veteran is a shutdown defender, often drawing the opponent's best player. Holiday doesn't post flashy offensive numbers (averaging 16 points per game over his career), and he played much of his time with the New Orleans Pelicans in the shadow of superstar Anthony Davis before Davis was traded to the Lakers in 2019. Still, when Holiday is on the floor, his team is better.

Holiday had his best season as a pro in 2018–19. While Davis was dealing with the fallout of publicly requesting a trade, Holiday elevated his game. He posted career highs in points per game (21.7) and rebounds per game (5). Holiday's 2018–19 season was filled with plenty of highlights, but an early season game at home against the Brooklyn Nets personified his clutch play.

The Pelicans were trailing 115–114 with seven seconds to go as Holiday took the inbounds pass. He didn't panic. Instead, he worked his way to the top of the key. He began to drive the lane, then pulled up at the foul line and took the fadeaway jumper. He buried the shot and the Pelicans won, 116–115!

JEWELL LOYD

The Seattle Storm invested the first overall draft pick on Jewell Loyd in 2015, and Loyd hasn't disappointed. The year before she arrived in Seattle, the Storm had a record of 12–22 and missed the playoffs. Just four seasons later, Loyd led the Storm to the WNBA Championship!

The former Notre Dame standout became a dependable player for the Storm, playing in every game of her first four years in the league. The five-foot-ten guard has averaged over 15 points per game in her career. She is also money from the free-throw line. In a 2015 game against the Washington Mystics, Loyd set a franchise record by hitting 14–14 from the line. Her perfection helped the Storm come back from a 14-point deficit to win the game.

Free throws are nice, but legacies are made in the playoffs. In the 2018 Finals, Loyd came out on fire. She led all scorers in Game 1 with 23 points. Thanks to her dominance, the Storm won the game and never looked back. They swept the Mystics 3–0 to take the title. They won a second WNBA Championship in 2020.

Legendary Great **SHOOTING GUARD**

MICHAEL JORDAN

Dozens of books and documentaries have chronicled every aspect of Jordan's life on and off the basketball court. If he isn't the greatest basketball player that ever lived, then he is standing just a half-step behind LeBron James.

Many fans already have an appreciation for the man they call simply "MJ." Rather than trying to single out a game or two from the endless buzzer beaters and monster performances of his career, let's instead get a sense of the impact he had on the world around him.

His legend transcends generations. His high-flying dunks, with tongue sticking out, were often imitated and rarely replicated. He had millions of kids on playgrounds around the world trying to "Be like Mike." Every time he touched the basketball, fans expected something special to happen. It seemed like there was no shot he couldn't make. Half-court buzzer beaters were a regular occurrence. He was equally comfortable at fast-paced dribbling between opponents as he was gracefully arcing a long-distance three-pointer.

In a game that is incredibly fast, Jordan made it seem leisurely, almost easy at times. He often looked like he had another gear the other players on the court were missing, as though he could see three moves ahead and anticipate what his opponent was going to do next. He was, for many years, unstoppable.

Jordan was such an athletic talent that he took a season off mid-career and played professional baseball. (He signed a minor-league contract with the Chicago White Sox in 1994.) Jordan knocked in 51 runs, stole 30 bases, and sold out every stadium he played in. Then, as though he never left, he returned to the Chicago Bulls and led them to three titles over the next four seasons.

But legendary players are measured beyond the court as well. Jordan has donated tens of millions of dollars to charities. He has supported children's programs and worked to provide opportunities for the disadvantaged. He built and funded a Boys & Girls Club in Chicago, which he named after his late father.

One of Jordan's most enduring gestures came in 2001. After the September 11 terrorist attacks, Jordan announced he was donating his entire salary for the 2001–02 season to support the families who lost loved ones in the attacks. At the time, Jordan said simply, "It's my way of giving back and hopefully aiding those in need during a terrible time."

Of course MJ's value as a legend can't be summed up in a few stats and game highlights—but here is a taste of "Air Jordan" by the numbers: 32,292 points; 6,672 rebounds; 5,633 assists; six NBA Championship titles; five league MVP awards; and six Finals MVP awards.

Jordan led the league in scoring 10 times and holds the record for the most playoff games scoring 40 or more points. He did it an incredible 38 times! Today he is known as the former owner of the Charlotte Bobcats and the namesake of Air Jordan shoes, but for a generation of basketball fans, he was simply the greatest.

Create Your Own
FANTASY TEAM

RESOURCES

If you'd like to learn more about the game of basketball and these legendary players, please visit the following:

WEBSITES

NBA.com The official site of the NBA for the latest NBA scores, stats, and news

WNBA.com The official site of the WNBA

NCAA.com The official website of the National Collegiate Athletic Association

APPS

NBA app (iOS, Android, Windows Phone)

WNBA app (iOS, Android, Windows Phone)

REFERENCES

Note: All statistics used in the introductory boxes for each player as well as awards, all-star appearances, etc. were collected from www.basketball-reference.com unless otherwise noted. All NBA statistics are through the end of the 2022-23 season.

NBA CENTER: JOEL EMBIID

Behrens, Tanner. "Joel Embiid." Beyond the Single Story (blog), March 27, 2018. BeyondTheSingleStory.wordpress.com/2018/03/27/joel-embiid.

Decourcy, Mike. "Joel Embiid's Pursuit of Hoops Greatness Not Just a Dream." Sporting News, January 22, 2014. SportingNews.com/us/ncaa-basketball/news/joel-embiids-pursuit-of-hoops-greatness-not-just-a-dream/wxyk1v6zv97t1pep47qnkyv1y.

House of Highlights. "Joel Embiid Postgame Press Conference | Sixers vs Heat - Game 3 | April 19, 2018 | 2018 NBA Playoffs." YouTube, April 19, 2018. YouTube.com/watch?v=QbQgkn9Tg2w.

Kansas Athletics. "Joel Embiid." KUAthletics.com/roster/joel-embiid.

WNBA CENTER: BRITTNEY GRINER

Baylor University. "Brittney Griner." BaylorBears.com/sports/womens-basketball/roster/brittney-griner/3266.

ESPN. "Brittney Griner discusses being gay." April 18, 2013. ESPN.com/wnba/story/_/id/9185633/brittney-griner-comes-says-just-are.

HuffPost. "Brittney Griner, Openly Gay WNBA Star, Opens Up About Bullying and Being a Role Model." Last modified February 2, 2016. HuffPost.com/entry/brittney-griner-bullying_n_3617907?guccounter=1.

Jordan, Jason. "Brittney Griner's HS coach says she'll go down as the greatest of all time." High School Sports (*USA Today*), March 19, 2015. USATodayHSS.com/2015/brittney-griner-phoenix-mercury-griner-brittney-griner-dunk-nimitz-brittney-griner-wnba.

Rohlin, Melissa. "WNBA's Brittney Griner has learned to rise above it all." *Los Angeles Times*, July 17, 2013. LATimes.com/sports/la-xpm-2013-jul-17-la-sp-brittney-griner-20130718-story.html.

Tapper, Christina M. "Baylor Superstar Brittney Griner Talks About When She Was a Kid." *Sports Illustrated Kids*, March 22, 2013. SIKids.com/from-the-mag/brittney-griner-being-kid.

HONORABLE MENTIONS

ANTHONY DAVIS

ESPN. "Anthony Davis." ESPN.com/nba/player/_/id/6583/anthony-davis.

Wells, Adam. "Report: Anthony Davis Traded to Lakers for Lonzo Ball, Brandon Ingram, More." *Bleacher Report*, June 15, 2019. BleacherReport.com/articles/2755098-report-anthony-davis-traded-to-lakers-for-lonzo-ball-brandon-ingram-more.

NIKOLA JOKIĆ

Goldberg, Rob. "Nikola Jokic, Nuggets Reportedly to Agree to 5-Year, $148M Contract Extension." *Bleacher Report*, June 30, 2018. BleacherReport.com/articles/2782863-nikola-jokic-nuggets-reportedly-to-agree-to-5-year-148m-contract-extension.

LEGENDARY GREAT: KAREEM ABDUL-JABBAR

Van Dusen, Ryan. "Kareem Abdul-Jabbar - 1989 NBA Finals Highlights (42 Years Old)." YouTube, 4:17, August 10, 2016. YouTube.com/watch?v=JwTyxXPr8gY&t=256s.

NBA SMALL FORWARD: KAWHI LEONARD

Abrams, Jonathan. "The Making of Kawhi Leonard, the Silent Superstar." Bleacher Report, April 4, 2017. BleacherReport.com/articles/2700300-the-making-of-kawhi-leonard-the-silent-superstar.

Ford, Chad. "Pacers acquire guard George Hill." ESPN, June 23, 2011. ESPN.com/nba/draft2011/news/story?id=6698432.

Schwartz, Nick. "What's going on with Kawhi Leonard: A strange timeline." For the Win (*USA Today*), July 18, 2018. FTW.USAToday.com/2018/07 /whats-going-on-with-kawhi-leonard-a-strange-timeline.

Uggetti, Paolo. "The Real L.A. Stories of Kawhi Leonard and Paul George." The Ringer, October 3, 2019. TheRinger.com/nba-preview/2019/10/3 /20895966/kawhi-leonard-paul-george-los-angeles-clippers-stories -growing-up.

WNBA SMALL FORWARD: ELENA DELLE DONNE

Brodesser-Akner, Taffy. "The Audacity of Height." ESPN, November 22, 2016. ESPN.com/espn/feature/story/_/page/espnw-delledonne161122 /chicago-sky-elena-delle-donne-spent-years-learning-accept-height.

Byrum, Tyler. "Elena Delle Donne wins her first championship despite three herniated discs in her back." NBC Sports, October 10, 2019. NBCSports.com/washington/wizards/elena-delle-donne-wins-her -first-championship-despite-three-herniated-discs-her-back.

Associated Press. "Elena Delle Donne returning to U.S. after Lyme disease flare-up." ESPN.com/wnba/story/_/id/18552312/elena-delle-donne -heading-back-us-china-lyme-disease-flare-up?device=featurephone.

Ginsburg, David. "Delaware star Delle Donne has no regrets about leaving UConn." *Star Tribune*, March 21, 2013. StarTribune.com/delaware-star -delle-donne-has-no-regrets-about-leaving-uconn/199457221.

Maloney, Jack. "WNBA Finals 2019: Elena Delle Donne's back injury has massive impact on Mystics' Game 2 loss to Sun." CBS Sports, October 1, 2019. CBSSports.com/wnba/news/wnba-finals-2019-elena-delle-donnes -back-injury-has-massive-impact-on-mystics-game-2-loss-to-sun.

Schroeder, Jessa. "'I love a woman, it is no big deal': WNBA star Elena Delle Donne marries girlfriend Amanda Clifton in lavish ceremony." *Daily Mail*, November 4, 2017. DailyMail.co.uk/news/article-5049019 /WNBA-star-Elena-Delle-Donne-marries-Amanda-Clifton.html.

Smith, Bryan. "The New Superstar in Town." *Chicago*, May 16, 2016. www .ChicagoMag.com/Chicago-Magazine/June-2016/Elena-Delle-Donne.

Spruill, Tamryn. "Hoops Happening: Elena Delle Donne, 'Uninterrupted': 'Women aren't valued the same way that men are in the workforce.'" Swish Appeal (SB Nation), October 16, 2018. SwishAppeal.com/2018 /10/16/17976324/elena-delle-donne-nba-wnba-pay-equity-uninterrupted -maverick-carter.

Voepel, Mechelle. "Family comes first for Delle Donne, even during WNBA championship run." ESPN, October 7, 2019. ESPN.com/wnba /story/_/id/27792827/family-comes-first-delle-donne-even-wnba -championship-run.

HONORABLE MENTIONS

JIMMY BUTLER

NBA. "Reports: Minnesota Timberwolves trade Jimmy Butler to 76ers. "November 10, 2018. NBA.com/article/2018/10/04/report -minnesota-timberwolves-trade-butler-76ers.

Rapp, Timothy. "Jimmy Butler Talks 76ers Tenure, Says Some Teammates Didn't Work as Hard as Him." *Bleacher Report*, November 27, 2019. BleacherReport.com/articles/2864509-jimmy-butler-talks-76ers -tenure-says-some-teammates-didnt-work-as-hard-as-him.

KLAY THOMPSON

Goldberg, Rob. "Warriors Rumors: Klay Thompson Ready to Agree on 5-Year, $190M Contract with GS." *Bleacher Report*, June 26, 2019. BleacherReport.com/articles/2842944-warriors-rumors-klay -thompson-ready-to-agree-on-5-year-190m-contract-with-gs.

Shapiro, Michael. "Watch: Klay Thompson Sets NBA Record with 14 Threes vs. Bulls." *Sports Illustrated*, October 29, 2018. SI.com/nba /2018/10/30/klay-thompson-nba-record-14-threes.

MAYA MOORE

Nelson, Ryne. "Maya Moore Talks Motivation, Offseason and Dominant Minnesota Lynx Run." *SLAM*, September 26, 2018. SlamOnline.com /wnba/maya-moore-appreciative-dominant-minnesota-lynx-run.

LEGENDARY GREAT: LARRY BIRD

Gelso, Nick. "Larry Bird: The Sudden and Saddening Demise Of a Basketball Legend." Bleacher Report, July 31, 2009. BleacherReport.com/articles/228427-larry-bird-the-sudden-and-saddening-demise-of-a-basketball-legend.

NBA POWER FORWARD: LEBRON JAMES

Gaines, Cork. "LEBRON JAMES: How the king of the NBA spends his millions." Business Insider, May 10, 2019. BusinessInsider.com/how-lebron-spends-his-money-2016-6.

Helfand, Zach. "LeBron James Never Forgot Where He Came from, and They Never Forgot Him." *Los Angeles Times*, October 27, 2014. LATimes.com/sports/nba/la-sp-lebron-james-akron-20141028-story.html.

House of Highlights. "The Game MASKED LeBron James BECAME a LEGEND 2014.03.03 vs Bobcats - 61 Points, EPIC NIGHT!" YouTube, August 12, 2018. YouTube.com/watch?v=O5PRGB1Khts.

House of Highlights. "LeBron James Back-To-Back Championship, Game 7 Highlights vs Spurs 2013 Finals - 37 Pts, CLUTCH HD." YouTube, June 14, 2018. YouTube.com/watch?v=hDDzmksK4fw.

House of Highlights. "LeBron James First NBA Game, Full Highlights vs Kings (2003.10.29) - MUST WATCH Debut! HD." YouTube, June 19, 2018. YouTube.com/watch?v=JLjH0rrNFeU.

NBA. "LeBron James becomes first player in NBA history with triple-doubles vs. 30 teams." November 19, 2019. NBA.com/article/2019/11/20/lebron-james-becomes-first-post-triple-double-vs-30-teams.

Saslow, Eli. "Lost stories of LeBron, part 1." ESPN, October 17, 2013. ESPN.com/nba/story/_/id/9825052/how-lebron-james-life-changed-fourth-grade-espn-magazine.

WNBA POWER FORWARD: CANDACE PARKER

Nesfeder, Mary Paige. "WNBA Star Candace Parker Doesn't Want To Be One Of The Boys." Refinery29, June 21, 2019. Refinery29.com/en-us/candace-parker-wnba-gender-equality-basketball-interview.

USA Basketball. "Before They Made It: Candace Parker." March 21, 2014. USAB.com/news-events/news/2014/03/before-they-made-it-candace -parker.aspx.

Women's Basketball Daily. "WNBA Final Game 5 Los Angeles Sparks Minnesota Lynx 20 10 16." YouTube, December 18, 2016. YouTube.com /watch?v=zmS3fds64ms.

HONORABLE MENTIONS

GIANNIS ANTETOKOUNMPO

Goodman, Peter S. "Giannis Antetokounmpo Is the Pride of a Greece That Shunned Him." *New York Times*, May 3, 2019. NYTimes .com/2019/05/03/sports/giannis-antetokounmpo-greece.html.

BLAKE GRIFFIN

Daniels, Tim. "Blake Griffin Traded to Pistons for Avery Bradley, Tobias Harris and More." *Bleacher Report*, January 29, 2018. BleacherReport .com/articles/2614395-report-blake-griffin-traded-to-pistons-for-avery -bradley-tobias-harris-more.

Love, Ryan. "Pistons doomsday scenario: What if Blake Griffin can't come back?" FanSided. January 11, 2019. PistonPowered.com/2019 /11/01/pistons-doomsday-scenario-what-if-blake-griffin-cant-come-back.

NBA. "Blake Griffin Sets a NEW Career High 50 Points vs Sixers | October 23, 2018." YouTube, October 23, 2018. YouTube.com /watch?v=vxYBsUdosGo.

LEGENDARY GREAT: TIM DUNCAN

NBA. "Tim Duncan's San Antonio Spurs Jersey Retirement." YouTube, December 19, 2016. YouTube.com/watch?v=WNobXXMlrQk.

NBA POINT GUARD: STEPHEN CURRY

Becker, Jon. "Remember when Stephen Curry's ankle injuries threatened his career?" *The Mercury News*, last modified December 6, 2017. MercuryNews.com/2017/12/05/remember-when-stephen-currys-ankle -injuries-threatened-his-career.

Davis, Scott. "Stephen Curry shared an anecdote that shows how unlikely his NBA ascent has been." Business Insider, June 9, 2017. BusinessInsider .com/stephen-curry-high-school-unlikely-nba-career-2017-6.

TODAY. "Stephen Curry Responds to Being Called 'The Greatest Basketball Player of All Time': Full Interview." YouTube, 19:46, April 3, 2019. YouTube .com/watch?v=6S25PgJshPc&t=1186s.

WNBA POINT GUARD: SUE BIRD

Associated Press. "Bird becomes first guard to go No. 1." ESPN. April 19, 2002. ESPN.com/wnba/news/2002/0419/1371034.html.

Classic Basketball. "2001 Big East Championship Notre Dame vs Connecticut." YouTube, January 7, 2015. YouTube.com/watch?v =swZsMh3qs60.

Griffus, Annette. "NEW YORK 78, SEATTLE 61: Storm learn from, and lose to, Liberty." *Kitsap Sun*, May 31, 2002. Products.KitsapSun.com /archive/2002/05-31/0060_new_york_78__seattle_61__storm_le.html.

Ramachandran, Preetha. "WNBA star Sue Bird discusses sports equality at event." *The Chronicle*, September 17, 2019. DukeChronicle.com /article/2019/09/wnba-sue-bird-sports-equality-duke-university.

Seymour, Emma. "The Danger of Low Pay in the WNBA." *Ms.*, April 23, 2019. MsMagazine.com/2019/04/23/the-danger-of-low-pay-in-the-wnba.

HONORABLE MENTIONS

RUSSELL WESTBROOK

Ellentuck, Matt. "There's only 1 winner in the blockbuster Russell Westbrook trade to the Rockets." *SB Nation*, July 12, 2019. SBNation .com/2019/7/12/20691259/russell-westbrook-trade-rockets -chris-paul-winners-losers.

NBA. "Westbrook averages triple-double for third straight season." April 5, 2019. NBA.com/article/2019/04/05/westbrook-averages-triple-double -third-straight-season.

KYRIE IRVING

House of Highlights. "Kyrie Irving AMAZING Brooklyn Nets Debut Full Highlights vs Timberwolves (2019.10.23) - 50 Points!" YouTube, October 23, 2019. YouTube.com/watch?v=B1r6tgpxEwk.

COURTNEY VANDERSLOOT

Basketball Reference. "WNBA Year-by-Year Leaders and Records for Assists Per Game." Basketball-Reference.com/wnba/leaders/ast_per_g_yearly.html.

Kenney, Madeline. "Sky point guard Courtney Vandersloot earns third consecutive peak performer award." *Chicago Sun Times*, September 9, 2019. ChicagoSunTimes.com/chicago-sky-and-wnba/2019/9/9/20857600/sky-pg-courtney-vandersloot-earns-third-consecutive-peak-performer-award.

LEGENDARY GREAT: MAGIC JOHNSON

House of Highlights. "Rookie Magic Johnson Full Game 6 Highlights vs 76ers (1980 NBA Finals) - 42 Pts, 15 Reb, FINALS MVP!" YouTube, August 14, 2018. YouTube.com/watch?v=H906s1BZu-Y.

NBA SHOOTING GUARD: JAMES HARDEN

Associated Press. "James Harden gets $80 million." ESPN, October 31, 2012. ESPN.com/nba/story/_/id/8577246/james-harden-houston-rockets-agree-five-year-80-million-contract.

ESPN. "James Harden 'happy' he gave Madison Square Garden career-high 61 points in Rockets' win | NBA Sound." YouTube, January 23, 2019. YouTube.com/watch?v=Q426OCIx6uw.

House of Highlights. "James Harden EPIC Game-Winning Shot | Rockets vs Warriors - January 3, 2019." YouTube, January 4, 2019. YouTube.com/watch?v=L2g4RtMj2Ss.

Spears, Marc J. "Rockets' James Harden and His Mom on How Sports Shaped the MVP Candidate." The Undefeated, May 5, 2017. TheUndefeated.com/features/rockets-james-harden-and-mom-sports-shaped-mvp-candidate.

WNBA SHOOTING GUARD: DIANA TAURASI

Killian, Tyler. "Diana Taurasi to sit out 2015 WNBA season after accepting Russian team offer." *USA Today*, February 3, 2015. USAToday.com /story/sports/wnba/mercury/2015/02/03/diana-taurasi-to-miss-2015 -season/22816013.

Staff. "Phoenix Mercury earn third WNBA title, defeating Chicago Sky 87–82." Hoopfeed, September 13, 2014. HoopFeed.com/content/2014/09 /phoenix-mercury-earn-third-wnba-title-defeating-chicago-sky-87-82.

Taurasi, Diana. "Just a Kid from Chino." The Players' Tribune, September 3, 2015. ThePlayersTribune.com/en-us/articles/just-a-kid-from-chino.

Thakker, Krishna. "Diana Taurasi Breaks WNBA Scoring Record." *Fortune*, June 19, 2017. Fortune.com/2017/06/19/diana-taurasi-wnba-scoring-record.

HONORABLE MENTIONS

DONOVAN MITCHELL

NBA on ESPN. "[FULL] Quin Snyder says he doesn't view Donovan Mitchell as a rookie | NBA on ESPN." YouTube, April 15, 2018. YouTube.com/watch?v=RHb_3P0Mhug.

JRUE HOLIDAY

House of Highlights. "Jrue Holiday GAME-WINNER | Nets vs Pelicans | October 26, 2018 | 2018-19 NBA Season." YouTube, October 26, 2018. YouTube.com/watch?v=3K0gDRK4_RQ.

JEWELL LOYD

Basketball Reference. "Jewell Loyd WNBA Stats." Basketball-Reference .com/wnba/players/l/loydje01w.html.

Basketball Reference. "2014 Seattle Storm Stats." Basketball-Reference .com/wnba/teams/SEA/2014.html.

Evans, Jayda. "Rookie Jewell Loyd leads the way as Storm beats Mystics, 69-59." *The Seattle Times*, August 30, 2015. SeattleTimes.com/sports/storm/rookie-loyd-leads-the-way-as-storm-beats-mystics-69-59.

WNBA. "Emerald City: Seattle Selects Loyd With No. 1 Overall Pick." April 16, 2015. WNBA.com/draft2015.

WNBA. "WNBA Playoffs 2018." WNBA.com/playoffs2018.

LEGENDARY GREAT: MICHAEL JORDAN

Boys & Girls Clubs of Chicago. "James R. Jordan Boys & Girls Club." BGCC.org/jordan-club.

CNN.com/U.S. "Jordan to donate his salary for relief efforts." October 17, 2001. http://edition.cnn.com/2001/US/10/17/rec.jordan.salary/.

INDEX

ACKNOWLEDGMENTS

It takes a village to build a book, and it takes an even bigger village to build a writer who builds a book. Thanks to the many people who have helped me along the way, both in my career as a writer and specifically on this project. There are too many to name, but I'll name a few anyway: Jack Callahan, the teacher who first made me believe I could be a writer; John F. J. Sullivan, the editor who took a chance on a kid with no training and no experience and gave me my first byline; Bram Hepburn, with whom I have a cherished 30-year friendship; Tim O'Shei, my friend and mentor, who introduced me to my first book editor and opened the door for me to be here writing this book today; Dr. Michael I. Niman, the most influential professor of my collegiate career at Buffalo State College, whose classes made me both a better researcher and a stronger writer; my good friend Jerry Wohlleber, who offered invaluable late-night advice during this project, even if we still fiercely debate whether the G.O.A.T. is MJ or LeBron (for the record, it's LeBron); my editor, David Lytle, and the team at Callisto Media; and finally, my mom, Christine Chandler. Though she left this world a year ago, the lessons she taught me and the love she gave me shape every word I write today. Without her, none of this would have ever been possible.

ABOUT THE AUTHOR

MATT CHANDLER is the author of more than 55 nonfiction books. He writes extensively about all types of sports and athletes. His *Sports Illustrated Kids* book, *Side-by-Side Baseball Stars: Comparing the Game's Greatest Players*, was selected by the American Society of Journalists and Authors for its 2015 Young Adult Outstanding Book Award. Matt is a former newspaper journalist and six-time New York Press Association award-winner. He lives in New York with his wife, Amber; his children, Zoey and Ollie; and Lola the dog and Sam the bird. You can learn more about his work at MattChandlerWriting.com.